ACTION RESEARCH
TO IMPROVE
SCHOOL PRACTICES

*A publication of the Horace Mann-Lincoln
Institute of School Experimentation
Teachers College, Columbia University*

STEPHEN M. COREY
*Horace Mann-Lincoln Institute
of School Experimentation
Teachers College
Columbia University*

Action Research

To Improve

School Practices

Bureau TEACHERS COLLEGE
of Publications COLUMBIA UNIVERSITY
NEW YORK
1953

Copyright, 1953, by Teachers College
Columbia University

Printed in the United States of America

Foreword

Research is of great importance to a profession. It is only through research that knowledge is increased and a basis for improved practice provided. Without the continuing impact of research findings, procedures become stereotyped, and the profession rapidly takes on the characteristics of a trade.

Although schools have long been established, the professionalization of teaching is of recent origin. In the effort to develop a sound basis for professional activity, research has received considerable emphasis in educational literature and in programs of teacher preparation. Yet any realistic appraisal will reveal that all too little educational practice is consciously grounded on research. The greatest influence on the teaching practices of too many teachers is still the methods by which they themselves were taught. One of the fundamental needs in strengthening education is the development of a more adequate research basis.

Educational research over the years has rather extensively adopted the concepts of procedure developed in the physical sciences. As a consequence, the laboratory-controlled situation has been the ideal widely sought. Thus research has tended to be rather far removed from the daily activities of the classroom teacher, the supervisor, and the school principal. The view has been gaining acceptance that this condition is an unsound one. While certain kinds of problems can be solved only by highly trained research specialists, other problems of equal importance can be solved only as teachers, supervisors, and principals become researchers. This represents a highly important extension of the role of research in education, and it requires some important developments in research procedures.

Professor Corey has analyzed with great clarity the elements in this extended concept of research. Further, he has provided illustrations of how this concept operates from a variety of experiences. His treatment should prove of great value to all educational workers in school situations who wish to improve their practice. It will also be found highly suggestive by those members of faculties of Education who teach research methods to classroom teachers and others not primarily research specialists.

HOLLIS L. CASWELL

Preface

This short book has been written because of three beliefs. Some would say that they are more than beliefs, being in the nature of well-established facts. But since I do not care to argue that distinction here, I shall call them beliefs.

The first is that we are now feeling only the beginnings of the effect that modern science and technology will have on our daily lives. This is true even though the consequences of discovery and invention, of man's conquest of nature, are already affecting, in some fashion or other, everything we do and are. We may shut our eyes and say, "This far and no further," but the forces that we have loosed are not so easily held in check. And they are cumulative in their effects. We have no choice but to learn to live with the changes that scientists and engineers have brought about in our ways of living and earning a living. We must change to survive, and in many respects our lives may be the richer.

The second belief reflects my understanding of the role of the school in a culture that, whether we wish it to or not, is changing dramatically. Unless formal education makes a big difference in the success with which boys and girls, and men and women, are able to make the adjustments they must make in an era of change, the education is not worth very much. Six billion dollars a year is too much to spend for it. If the lives we lead and shall lead are marked by change as they never have been before, education must change too, inevitably. The useful must be kept, and the testing of what was once useful and of what may be more useful must be continuous and thoughtful.

This leads to the question, Who will do the testing? Who will decide what must be kept and what must go and what must be added?

I have lost much of the faith I once had in the consequences of asking only the professional educational investigator to study the schools and to recommend what they should do. Incorporating these recommendations into the behavior patterns of practitioners involves some problems that so far have been insoluble. This leads to my third belief: Most of the study of what should be kept in the schools and what should go and what should be added must be done in hundreds of thousands of classrooms and thousands of American communities. The studies must be undertaken by those who may have to change the way they do things as a result of the studies. Our schools cannot keep up with the life they are supposed to sustain and improve unless teachers, pupils, supervisors, administrators, and school patrons continuously examine what they are doing. Singly and in groups, they must use their imaginations creatively and constructively to identify the practices that must be changed to meet the needs and demands of modern life, courageously try out those practices that give better promise, and methodically and systematically gather evidence to test their worth.

This is the process I call action research. I hold no especial brief for the name, but it has some currency and is sufficiently descriptive. What I will talk about is research that is undertaken by educational practitioners because they believe that by so doing they can make better decisions and engage in better actions.

Chapter I differentiates action research from traditional educational research. Chapter II describes and illustrates the process of action research. Chapter III reproduces two action research studies, one having to do with a supervisory problem, the other with an attempt to improve classroom teaching. In Chapter IV the relativity of research quality is considered, and then, in Chapter V, some of the conditions favorable to action-oriented educational experimentation are described. Chapter VI is a report of a graduate seminar that employed action research as a learning method. The main argument of the book concludes with a chapter in which some statistical problems faced in action research are considered and a study of the validity of generalizing from action research findings is described. The final chapter is a brief summary and concluding statement. Readers who are in a hurry will find that this final chapter is the book in capsule form.

The substance of most of the chapters has appeared in articles in professional journals. Each of these earlier statements of mine has been expanded and rewritten, but I am indebted for permission to use them to *Educational Administration and Supervision, Educational Leadership, The Journal of Educational Psychology, The School Review,* and *Teachers College Record.*

I have learned much of what I know about research undertaken by practitioners to improve their decisions and actions from groups in the field with which I have worked, and from my research associates in the Horace Mann-Lincoln Institute of School Experimentation. Arno A. Bellack, Alvin J. Bernstein, Hollis L. Caswell, Dale C. Draper, Arthur W. Foshay, Paul M. Halverson, George R. Hudson, Arthur T. Jersild, Richard E. Lawrence, Howard Leavitt, Gordon N. Mackenzie, Alice Miel, Matthew B. Miles, A. Harry Passow, Donald E. Super, and Charles F. Warnath—all present or former members of the Institute staff—as well as Jean D.

Grambs, of Stanford University, Glen Burch, of the Ford Foundation, and Willie Holdsworth, of the University of Texas, have read all or parts of the book in manuscript and have made many helpful suggestions. It should not be inferred that these people agree with everything that is said. Nor should it be inferred that this book is a statement of Institute rationale or policy. We do our work under a broad charter, and within its limits there is room for many kinds of research and experimentation. The staff would agree, however, that our work as action research consultants has been a continuing Institute emphasis.

Reference notes are liberally used in the text, but they are handled in a way somewhat different from that customary in educational books. In the Notes placed at the end of chapters I comment on the references that are consecutively numbered throughout each chapter, develop some ideas a bit further than I cared to in the text itself, and insert a number of quotations. These Notes are not essential to following the argument.

The preparation of this book has been expedited by the careful and conscientious help of Miss Nancy Montgomery, supervising secretary for the Horace Mann-Lincoln Institute of School Experimentation. I hereby express my thanks to her.

STEPHEN M. COREY
Horace Mann-Lincoln Institute
of School Experimentation
Teachers College, Columbia University

Contents

Foreword *by Hollis L. Caswell*	v
Preface	vii
I Research in education	1
Traditional Educational Research	1
Research for Practitioners	6
Distinctions between Traditional and Action Research	8
Action Research and Democratic Values	17
Conclusion	17
Notes to Chapter I	19
II The action research process	25
Decisions and Prediction of Consequences	26
The Action Hypothesis	27
An Illustrative Action Research	30
Action Research and Cooperation	36
Conclusion	40
Notes to Chapter II	42
III Two action research studies	46
"Action Research to Improve Teacher Planning Meetings" *by Mary Neel Smith*	47
"We Tested Some Beliefs about the Biographical Method" *by Tressa Banks, Edgar*	

S. Farley, Oscar Powers, Floyd Vandermeer, Robert Waldorf, and Stephen M. Corey 61

IV COMMON SENSE AND ACTION RESEARCH 71
    Problem Solving: The Method of Common Sense 72
    Problem Solving: The Method of Action Research 78
    Conclusion 83
    Notes to Chapter IV 85

V CONDITIONS FAVORABLE TO ACTION RESEARCH 86
    Freedom to Admit Limitations 87
    Opportunities to Invent 91
    Encouragement to "Try It Out" 94
    Improvement in Methods of Group Work 95
    Concern with Obtaining Evidence 100
    Time and Resources for Experimentation 101
    Conclusion 103
    Notes to Chapter V 105

VI ACTION RESEARCH AS A WAY TO LEARN 107
    Identifying Group Needs for Self-Training in Human Relations 110
    Practicing Sensitivity to Hurt Feelings 113
    Evaluating the Seminar Sessions 118
    Evaluating the Seminar as a Whole 120

VII ACTION RESEARCH, STATISTICS AND THE SAMPLING PROBLEM 126
    The Effect of Courses in Statistics 126
    Statistical Concepts and Operations for Experimenting Teachers 130
    Action Research and the Sampling Problem 132
    Notes to Chapter VII 140

VIII IN SUMMARY 141
BIBLIOGRAPHY 149
INDEX 157

ACTION RESEARCH
TO IMPROVE
SCHOOL PRACTICES

CHAPTER I

Research in Education*

The main contention in this chapter is that the scientific movement in education has had little effect on the way school practitioners—teachers, supervisors, and administrators—go about trying to solve their professional problems. The professional students of education, as distinguished from the practitioners, have taken over the scientific method and are disposed to guard research activities closely as their province. Some criticisms of this situation are elaborated, and the chapter concludes by contrasting, in a number of respects, traditional educational research with action research.

Traditional Educational Research

The scientific movement began to influence a few American educators about fifty years ago.[1]† Nothing exceedingly rigorous or experimental is meant by this use of the expression *scientific movement*. It merely refers to the dawning of a

---

* A number of the ideas developed in this chapter first appeared in "Action Research, Fundamental Research, and Educational Practices," *Teachers College Record*, 50:509-514, May 1949.

† Superior figures in the text refer to items in the Notes at the end of chapters.

realization that (1) pedagogical problems can be attacked somewhat objectively; (2) quantitative evidence rather than reference to authority or precedent can be used as a basis for many educational decisions; and (3) measurement of what school children have learned is not only possible but feasible.

This interest in using the method of scientific inquiry to reach better judgments about school practices was, for a number of reasons, closely related to the early history of psychology in this country. By 1900 American psychologists had indicated their inclination to use the experimental method of inquiry that had first been developed in Germany. The subject matter of their investigations and the interpretation of their research data, however, were strongly influenced by Darwin. As Boring has pointed out, "American psychology was to deal with the mind in use." (6, p. 494) *
In connection with their studies of "the mind in use," Cattell and others who had returned to America from their training in Germany were encouraged by their attempts to measure mental activities. Instruments and methods that could conveniently be used to get evidence of what was happening to children in schools were developed. The "mental" content, the emphasis on measurement, and especially the scientific method of experimentation, which characterized American psychology early in the century, appealed to people interested in teaching and learning.

No attempt will be made here to trace the history of the application of the scientific method to the study of educational problems, for that has been done elsewhere.[2] What will be commented on is the apparent fact that this objective approach, with its emphasis on quantification and the testing of promising hypotheses by experimentation, has not yet moved into the broad stream of educational practice.

* Numbers in parentheses refer to items in the Bibliography on p. 149-154.

In the twenties and early thirties some attempts were made to encourage teachers and other practical school people to conduct research.[3] The common view at that time, however, was that the research that was recommended for school practitioners was (*a*) a way of adding to the body of tested truths about education, or (*b*) a technique to help the professional researcher get the data he needed, or (*c*) training in problem solving for teachers. Little was said about research as a method by which practicing school people could improve their decisions and actions.[4]

One circumstance that helps explain why the scientific method of problem solving did not become an important part of educational practice was its early identification, for reasons that are various, with a much narrower sphere of interest. The method of science was adopted not by the *practitioners* but by the professional *students* of education. The university professors and the staff members of research bureaus are the ones who spoke and wrote, and who still speak and write, voluminously and persuasively about the science of education. What they write and say implies their belief that research, in any basic sense, is not an activity in which amateurs can engage. The standards that are established for "acceptable" research in the textbooks and courses on educational research methodology are high. Those who face practical problems in their teaching or supervision or administration are not disposed to think that they can approach these problems scientifically. Years must be spent in training before anyone is ready to be a scientific educator. A doctoral degree is almost a prerequisite.

At the present time most men and women who consider themselves educational researchers believe that it is the professional investigator, the *student* of education, who should be persistent and indefatigable in his scientific study of the problems *that other people must face*. Of the approximately nine hundred men and women who were affiliated with the

American Educational Research Association in 1952, few were practitioners in the sense in which the term is used here. Less than 10 per cent were supervisors, administrators, or principals. The number of elementary or secondary school classroom teachers who were members could be counted on the fingers of one hand. Professors of education and staff members of educational research bureaus predominated.

These students of education, not being the ones who normally make decisions and take action about practical school problems, assume an attitude toward the purpose of scientific inquiry similar to that of many other social scientists. It is argued that the chief justification for scientific investigations in education is the establishment of generalizations that can be stated as observed uniformities, explanatory principles, or scientific laws. Hypotheses are to be tested in such a way as to warrant conclusions extending beyond the populations or situations studied. The interest is in discovering "the truth" or coming as close to it as possible. Practicing school people are then to use this "truth" to improve the quality of education.

The conviction that research should be left to the disinterested professionals has a venerable tradition. People who want to improve social situations are not considered by the scientist to be sufficiently objective to be trusted as investigators. Applied to education, this means that a curriculum worker in service, whose job it is to help develop better school experiences for boys and girls, is not in a favorable position to conduct research. His evaluation activities should not be called research, or certainly not scientific research. He is too interested in the outcome.

The result of this attitude has been that the sequence of events in traditional educational research is usually somewhat as follows. First, an interesting and often an important question occurs to a group of investigators or, more frequently, to a single investigator. He may be, for example, a student of adolescent development, who wants to learn more about the relationship between football experience and the incidence of driving accidents. His hypothesis is that the excitement and risk involved in football reduce the need for the excitement and risk provided by driving an automobile recklessly. Customarily, the investigator would next make an exhaustive search of the literature to see what, if anything, other people had discovered and published about this relationship. If he found no answer to his question, or one that he thought inadequate, he would proceed to design and conduct an inquiry.

In all likelihood this investigator would have no intention of doing anything personally with the results of his study beyond publishing them and possibly suggesting their relevance to some theory about adolescent development. He probably would not be working with adolescents himself. In only a vague, general sense would he feel any obligation to reduce the frequency of car accidents involving adolescent drivers. He just wants to find the answer to a question that seems to him to be important and intriguing. Someone else may use the findings to modify practices if he cares to do so. This probably will be recommended in the last paragraph of the investigator's report. He himself, however, after he has conducted his study and interpreted and published his data, will go on to other things. He is a researcher and a student, not an educational practitioner.

This traditional attitude toward educational research should not be interpreted as implying that most professional investigators are unconcerned about practice. They seem to believe, however, that their published discoveries will, in due course and almost automatically, bring about change for the better. The fact that the professional researcher is rarely, if ever, actively engaged in trying to do something about the problem he is studying is cited as a virtue. Concern about practical action resulting from his research might contaminate his data, his experimental design, or his reputation with his peers. The assumption is that when people who are exceedingly well trained to investigate educational problems go about their inquiries scientifically and communicate their findings to practitioners, progress is inevitable. The role of teachers, supervisors, and administrators is to apply the results of the educational research they read or hear about.[5] The fact that these applications have been slow in coming seems not to have caused many professional educational investigators to question their conception of the relation between research and improvement of practice.[6]

During the past thirty or forty years this general attitude toward the study of educational problems has resulted in an amazing accumulation of research findings. The library shelves of teacher-training institutions are heavy with journals, monographs, and texts that report the studies of the scientific educational researchers. Each year the major American universities offering the doctorate in education add several hundred new doctoral researches to the published literature.

Research for Practitioners

The view that educational research is the prerogative of the professional students of education is a limited one. The method of scientific inquiry certainly has important implications not only for professional investigators but for others as well. The thesis of this book is that teachers, supervisors, and administrators would make better decisions and engage in more effective practices if they, too, were able and willing to conduct research as a basis for these decisions and practices. The process by which practitioners attempt to study their problems scientifically in order to guide, correct, and evaluate their decisions and actions is what a number of people have called action research.

The expression *action research* and the operations it implies come from at least two somewhat independent sources. One is the activities and writings of Collier during the period (1933–45) when he was Commissioner of Indian Affairs. Collier represented a group that was emphasizing the importance of social planning, and he insisted that "research and then more research is essential to the program . . . ." (18, p. 275) He used the expression *action research* and was convinced that "since the findings of research must be carried into effect by the administrator and the layman, and must be criticized by them through their experience, the administrator and the layman must themselves participate creatively in the research, impelled as it is from their own area of need." (18, p. 276)

The second source is Lewin and his students, many of whom have attempted to study human relations scientifically and to improve the quality of human relations as a consequence of their inquiries.[7] In the field of education, most of the practices of the evaluation staff of the Eight Year Study resemble action research closely.[8] Herrick (43) uses the expression *cooperative study* to mean much the same thing in connection with curriculum development. The report of the experimental programs sponsored by the Project in Intergroup Education of the American Council on Education (see Taba, Brady, and Robinson [75]) stresses a method of problem solving that includes most of the elements of action research. Wrightstone (79) uses the term *research-action* in describing one of the functions of curriculum bureaus.[9]

The school people who engage in action research are not disposed to make a neat distinction between scientific inquiry and educational practice. As has been said, this separation implies that if the researcher reports his findings to the practitioner, the latter will modify his practices to make them conform to the newly discovered data. There is some evidence, in addition to a great deal of thoughtful speculation about learning, which questions the effectiveness of this method of transforming knowledge into action.[10] Certainly much of the published information resulting from traditional educational research has had a disappointing effect on practice. Even those teachers or administrators who hear about or read some of these reports are often slightly if at all influenced by them. Sometimes the individual who conducts the investigation does not himself modify those of his practices that are questioned by his own data. That was not his intention. This is evident in the teaching methods of some professional researchers who have reported what are considered to be significant data about the learning process.

The point has already been made that the men and women who are active in traditional educational research are concerned about the slowness with which their research findings affect practice. They take part in meetings where serious thought is given to the lag between what is done in the schools and what research indicates should be done. Almost every year there are sectional meetings of the American Educational Research Association at which papers dealing with this problem are read. Sometimes these papers imply pique that teachers are so slow in using the fine research data lying around. More often the authors contend that the difficulty is largely one of inadequate communication. They say that if the research reports were only more lucidly written, or more copiously illustrated, or if the implications for practice were stated more clearly, teachers and other practitioners would be able to incorporate the findings into their professional behavior patterns.[11]

Distinctions between Traditional and Action Research

Influence on Educational Practices

It is almost certain that the difficulty is deeper than communication, and is related to important principles of learning. A teacher is most likely to change his ways of working with pupils when he accumulates and interprets information about these pupils because he wants to work more effectively with them. Reading the traditional research study, conducted by someone else and describing boys and girls in general, may help if he happens to see some relation between the research findings and the instructional problem he is facing. Of one thousand teachers who may hear about the results of a basic study of reading, for example, a few, whose personal experience corroborates these results, will be ready to apply them. Having an authority on their side may give them the support they need in order to try out some of their own ideas. These changes in practice, however, are more likely to occur if they are a consequence of inquiry in which the teacher has been involved and are based upon evidence he has helped to procure and interpret in his attempts to solve an instructional problem important to him.[12]

This argument about the way behavior is changed should not imply the caricature that often comes as a rejoinder. It does not mean that everyone has to learn everything for himself, the hard way, so to speak. In one sense, of course, he must do this because no one can learn for him. What is being emphasized, however, is that learning that changes behavior substantially is most likely to result when a person himself tries to improve a situation that makes a difference to him. He then does his best to obtain and interpret some evidence describing the consequences of his presumably more adequate practice. When he defines the problem, hypothesizes actions that may help him cope with it, engages in these actions, studies the consequences, and generalizes from them, he will more frequently internalize the experience than when all this is done for him by somebody else, and he reads about it. One reason for this is that in the course of his inquiry, which involves the testing of hypotheses in action, he will actually practice the changed behavior that he has decided is more promising. He will also practice whatever is involved in evaluating the consequences of this changed behavior. He does not read about these practices, he engages in them. And he learns what he does. Placing an exaggerated value on what may happen as a consequence of publishing traditional research studies of educational problems is one of the occupational diseases of pedagogues, who are strongly disposed to overestimate the extent to which reading will change behavior.

In considering the effect of traditional research on educational practices, it is helpful to view research-established generalizations as falling in two broad categories. In the first category are the generalizations that have implications for textbook writing and the production of other types of instructional materials, for school-building construction, and for the manufacture of school apparatus and equipment. In the second category are the findings that have implications for teacher-pupil relations, for teaching methods not a consequence of new materials, and for points of view.[13]

Research results in the first category seem to affect practices much faster than those in the second. One reason for this is that the kind of persuasion that must be engaged in if practitioners are to make better choices among alternative actions is less frequently involved. Kerosene lamps, for example, are hardly available any more for lighting schools. Choosing such lamps does not present a real alternative when plans are being made for new school buildings. Architects who would build a school as it would have been built in 1900 are not around. At least not many of them are around. Textbooks with a vocabulary load far exceeding the comprehension level of the children who will try to read them are harder to buy than they were twenty years ago. The same is true of books with type that strains the eyes unnecessarily. In these areas research findings have tended to restrict the field of choice, so that there is no alternative but to modify practice in accordance with the implications of research data. The fact that investigations in this first category usually result in products that can be sold for profit also helps to bring about more rapid change. The forces of advertising are powerful forces, and commerce thrives on genuine as well as presumed obsolescence.

The problem is quite different when research data have implications for improving teacher-pupil relations and therefore learning. Investigations indicating the importance of intrinsic motivation for useful learning suggest rather forcefully that pupils should be much more actively involved in planning and evaluating their own education than they now are. These research findings, however, even if read by teachers and, if necessary, "interpreted" for them, do not result in any appreciable restriction of choice among the various methods of teaching.

One specific illustration of the great lag between the implications of research findings in the second category and practice concerns the pattern of high school courses required for college entrance. Twenty-five years ago Douglass (36) conducted studies of the traditional research sort that demonstrated beyond a reasonable doubt that the particular subjects a young person took in high school had no detectable relationship to his college grades. These studies were published, and were available to anyone. But not much happened. Ten years later, as part of the Eight Year Study, Chamberlain and his associates (13) reported analogous and supporting data. Eight years after this, according to Redefer (67), very little had been done about their implications.[14]

This does not mean that no practical consequences resulted from these studies. But, measured against the assumptions regarding the process of change that underlie much of the traditional research in education, the consequences were insignificant. The action research program under way now in the state of Michigan, involving cooperative study and evaluation by most of the people who are affected by the proposed modifications, has already changed college entrance requirements in that state.[15] The information justifying these changes had been in the public domain, so to speak, for a long time. But because the people who themselves had to change did not participate in the accumulation and interpretation of this information, they were but slightly influenced by it.

Research Design and Criteria of Quality

There are distinctions between traditional research and action research other than those resulting from different conceptions about the way to bring about improvement in educational practices. One of them has to do with the inviolability of the experimental design. In traditional research careful thought is given to planning the design of an investigation before it is launched. This design is usually adhered to rigidly until the investigation has been completed. If, for example, an investigator were testing the hypothesis that units planned by teacher and pupils will result in better learning than the same units assigned comparable children without teacher-pupil planning, he would design his inquiry to last over a considerable period of time. Having committed himself to this predetermined design, he would be most reluctant to modify it. This would be true even if the results at the end of two months indicated that the teacher who was assigning to the second group of youngsters units that had been planned with the first group was running into serious difficulties.

The initial design of action research cannot be inviolable in this sense. The definition of the problem, the hypotheses to be tested, and the methods to be employed in testing the hypotheses undergo modification as interim results are validated or invalidated in practice and new hypotheses and methods are suggested by the developing situation. The very nature of action research makes it highly improbable that the investigator or investigators will know definitely and in advance the exact pattern of the inquiry that will develop. If an initial design is treated with too much respect, the researcher may not be sufficiently sensitive to the developing irrelevance of this design to the on-going action situation.

One implication of this discussion so far is that the quality of fundamental research and the quality of action research are to be judged by different criteria. The value of the former is determined by the amount of dependable knowledge it adds to that already recorded and available to anyone who wants to familiarize himself with it. The value of action research, on the other hand, is determined primarily by the extent to which findings lead to improvement in the practices of the people engaged in the research.

Generalizations Resulting from Research

Attention should be called to another difference between traditional and action research, which has received little notice. Conventional educational research is ordinarily designed so that generalizations can be extended to large populations. A crucial element in this design is the selection of subjects who will be representative of the larger population to which the generalizations are extended. Actually, many traditional researches in education violate two assumptions involved in the conventional textbook formulas used to determine the limits within which generalizations can be extrapolated. One assumption is that the parent population represents a normal distribution in respect to whatever abilities or capacities are central to the investigation. The other assumption is that the subjects studied represent a random sample from that normal population.[16]

The problems faced in generalizing from action research

are somewhat different from those faced in generalizing from traditional research. The action research inquiry is conducted by investigators studying a particular existing population. Whether or not it represents a random selection from a larger total population is rarely, if ever, considered. Action research is criticized because of this fact. It is said that whatever is found to be "true" about the children of School System A or the teachers of School System A cannot be considered "true" for a total population of boys and girls or a total population of teachers because the persons used as subjects do not represent a random sample from any known total population.

This criticism of action research calls attention to principles that must be attended to whenever generalizations are extended beyond the population providing evidence for their support. It should be recalled, however, that investigators engaged in action research are not attempting to establish generalizations applicable to groups of school children or teachers in other school systems. They are busy discovering generalizations that they hope will help them work more effectively with present and future populations of school children or teachers in the same situation as that in which the studies were conducted.

While this does not eliminate the necessity for extending generalizations from a sample population to a larger population, it does change the direction of the extension. In a real sense action research studies are undertaken not to make possible *lateral* extensions of generalizations but to make possible *vertical* extensions, with the vertical line going into the future. What this means is that if a third-grade teacher in School System X conducts action research to improve her practices and reaches certain conclusions, these conclusions have their greatest applicability to groups of third-grade youngsters that she may teach in the future in School System X.

If there is to be any assurance that the vertical extension of generalizations is justified, evidence must support a hypothesis that may be phrased as follows:

> The boys and girls a teacher has in the third grade in her school in 1953 are representative of, or a random sample from, the total population of boys and girls she will have in the third grade in this school system in 1954, 1955, 1956, and so on.

If this hypothesis can be supported—and Chapter VII describes the kind of evidence that is being used to find out whether or not it can be—the reasoning that has been developed to support the lateral extension of generalizations can also be used to support vertical extension, which is more appropriate to the spirit and intent of action research.

Research as a Cooperative Activity

An important personal qualification for action researchers in education is their skill in the cooperative study of problems. An individual teacher can engage in action research and sometimes does. But education as it is practiced in public schools is almost by definition a group activity, and there has been a great increase recently in the frequency with which practical educational problems are being studied by groups rather than individuals. Consequently, people who engage in action research must usually be able to work effectively with others who are also involved in the situation that is to be improved. Traditional research frequently involves team activity, but action research usually requires the joint effort of a group of people.

The importance of cooperation in action research will be discussed more fully in Chapters II and V. It will suffice here to illustrate the necessity for this cooperation when attempts are made to improve the curriculum.

If experiments are being conducted in a particular school

to develop a better program of general education, these experiments must take into account the ideas and experiences and expectations of pupils, teachers, administrators, and parents and other lay adults. All these people will ultimately influence and be influenced by the program. Unless the research undertaken to guide decisions and evaluate actions is cooperative, many important factors that have a bearing on the success of the general education program may be overlooked. Even more important, the research findings may never result in action. Writing about the importance of cooperative research as a means of influencing action, Lippitt says:

> One of the most promising . . . techniques for ensuring that data are communicated into action is so to organize consultant research operations that the group to be served, the potential consumers of the data, are collaborators in the planning, the measurement operations, and the analysis and interpretation of the data. (52, p. 9)

A failure to see the necessity for cooperation in curriculum research has marred the attempts of many communities to improve their schools. Too often several teachers have worked alone, conducting studies that resulted in what they believed were excellent changes in methods or materials. But because parents, too, had a stake in this new program, and because they had not been involved in the research and study that brought it into being, they misunderstood and objected to its aims and practices. An interesting history could be written of the birth, life, and death of many curriculum innovations. Often the cause of demise was not a lack of excellence in the innovation viewed in the abstract, but the resistance of powerful groups that had had no part in its development.[17]

Action Research and Democratic Values

It is common, in writing about the application of the scientific method to the study of educational problems, to stress the close relationship between this method and democracy as a way of life. Dewey (31) and others have written extensively in support of this relationship. Collier states that action research "has invariably operated to deepen our realization of the potentialities of the democratic way...." (18, p. 276) This argument is persuasive, but it is not elaborated here at all because the use of the method of science in the solution of practical educational problems can be adequately defended for its own sake. It is true, however, that extensive use of the method of science, especially in areas involving human relations, can be expected only in a relatively free, democratic society.[18]

Conclusion

This discussion of traditional and action research has stressed differentiation and separateness, and may have implied too sharp a distinction between the two kinds of inquiry. Actually they have much in common. The validity of any social research must be judged by its effect on human welfare. The individual interested in traditional educational research believes that the establishment and publication of enduring laws and principles will improve educational practices and hence human welfare. Any inquiry that neglects the generalizing process is limited in usefulness. The action researcher knows that he must generalize beyond his data because he never deals with the same situation twice. He is interested in applying his findings to next year's teachers or to next year's kindergarten children.

Traditional research in education and action research in

education are also alike in that each is difficult to do well. A great deal has been written in an attempt to improve the procedures of traditional research. Very little has been written, in the field of education, that will be particularly helpful to persons who are interested in action research. Most of the references to this kind of investigation have to do with attempts to improve human relations.

There is considerable justification for the belief that research methodology will not begin to have the influence that it might have on American education until thousands of teachers, administrators, and supervisors make more frequent use of the method of science in solving their own practical problems. But the method of science is not easy to employ, especially in an investigation of on-going activities. Not many of the people who are strongly committed to the scientific study of problems others face are disposed to be scientific when they try to improve their own day-to-day activities. Most of them continue to make decisions and engage in practices that are based on inadequate problem definition, subjective recall of evidence, and unsophisticated generalizing.

What this means is that those who are interested in seeing research contribute more substantially to the improvement of American education must do everything within their power to make a scientific attack on practical problems interesting, rewarding, and attractive to large numbers of people. The difference between the way most problems are handled and a more scientific treatment of them is relative (see Chapter IV). It is entirely possible to improve the clarity with which practical problems are identified, the creativeness with which more promising practices are hypothesized, the skill with which presumably better practices are implemented, the ingenuity with which evidence of the worth of the practices is obtained, and the penetration and sagacity of generalizations resulting from this evidence.

NOTES TO

CHAPTER I

1. Rice's studies (68) mark a convenient historical reference point for tracing the influence of the scientific movement on education. These studies first appeared in *The Forum* in 1897, under the title "The Futility of the Spelling Grind." In a book published in 1913 (69) he again reported some of his 1897 data and made interesting comments on their reception by educators. Although this book is forty years old and the studies on which much of it is based were conducted fifty-six years ago, the attitude toward a science of education and its promise is surprisingly modern.

2. Dewey's *The Sources of a Science of Education* (34) is a helpful philosophical statement of the meaning of the method of science for educators. Monroe and Engelhart (62, chap. xiv) treat briefly the development of a scientific attitude toward the study of education. These authors were most conscientious in ferreting out of the literature almost everything that had been written on any topic they considered. The chapter cited is twenty-two pages long and includes some sixty footnote references. Anyone who is interested in learning more about the history of the "science" of education will find a great deal of material in this chapter and in the books and articles cited in the footnotes.

3. A 1926 book by Buckingham, entitled *Research for Teachers,* was written "to show the teacher some of the things he can use in his work—things which have been developed not merely by appeal to principles, but primarily by methods of experimentation." (8, p. iv) A second purpose was "to show that the teacher has opportunities for research, which, if

seized, will not only powerfully and rapidly develop the technique of teaching, but will also react to vitalize and dignify the work of the individual teacher." (8, p. iv) Buckingham describes statistics that the modern teacher needs, methods of testing, new types of examinations, ways of grouping and classifying pupils, and techniques of individualizing instruction. He includes much helpful information about research tools and understandings, but the assumption seems to be that teachers will easily be able to relate these tools and techniques and understandings to their practical problems of instruction. Buckingham concludes that teacher research "would be desirable, even if no account were taken of the results as contributions to knowledge. The spirit of research among teachers would be justified merely in the reaction upon the teachers themselves." (8, p. 380)

4. Good, Barr, and Scates stress repeatedly how important it is for teachers to develop the habit of conducting research. In their Preface they say: "Although some field workers will make significant contributions to the store of educational knowledge as active participants in the production of research, the primary outcomes for the majority of field participants in educational research will be found in the training value of the problem-solving approach with an increased understanding of the educational process." (40, p. v) These authors go on to say: "The preceding paragraph should not be interpreted to mean that all field workers are to do research regardless of their training and qualifications. . . . Not all teachers will rise to the level of making scientific contributions to the study of education." (40, p. v) Here again it is implied that the chief reason for research by teachers is either its training value or its contribution to the great body of scientific information about education.

5. Monroe and Engelhart describe a third "audience" to which their text is addressed, which consists "of the consumers of educational research. These include superintendents, principals, supervisors, teachers, and others who endeavor to ascertain what research has accomplished in the field of educa-

tion, and to interpret the findings with respect to theory or practice." (62, p. v) Practitioners are not thought of as investigators.

6. In writing about time-diffusion patterns for educational innovations, Mort and Cornell summarize generalizations from charts describing the diffusion of nine such innovations as follows: "From these charts we may infer that it will take a half-century for the average adaptation to diffuse completely; it takes a third of a century after 3 per cent of the districts have made the introduction. Frequently there has been a long period of preparatory work in the community before the adaptation step is taken." (63, p. 53) Acceptance of the argument that changes in educational practices come very slowly need not, of course, imply agreement with the authors' calculation of the actual time required.

7. Students of Lewin emphasize the collaboration of men of science with men of action on action research teams. In the Preface to Lippitt's *Training in Community Relations* this statement appears: "Bringing together in a single cooperative adventure the skills and resources of both men of science, and men of action, this project is an example of 'action research.'" (52, p. ix)

8. See Eugene R. Smith, Ralph W. Tyler, and the evaluation staff (72).

9. Hopkins (44) comments on the differences in motivation ("need satisfaction") between pure, or basic or traditional, research and practical, or action, research. He stresses the importance of involving pupils in the action research process and paying particular attention to their reactions. He thinks of action research as a way of learning rather than a process that results in publication or reporting of "truths." Hopkins believes there is nothing new about action research and cites what he considers to have been substantially the same approach in curriculum improvement programs thirty years ago.

An interesting development, analogous to action research,

has resulted from World War II studies of operations in the British and American armed forces. This kind of inquiry has been called operations research, and is described by Kittel, of the Bell Telephone Laboratories, as "a scientific method for providing executives with a quantitative basis for decisions." (19, p. 2) Goodeve, of the British Iron and Steel Research Association, refers to operations research as "quantitative common sense." (19, p. 2)

10. Anderson and Gates (1) cite ten trends that have emerged within the past few years as psychologists have given greater and greater attention to the dynamics of learning. They comment on the increased importance attached to goal seeking and tension reduction. The yearbook in which this chapter appears repeatedly emphasizes how important it is for a learner to perceive the relationship between his needs and the knowledge or information available to him if this knowledge or information is to have an effect on his behavior.

Many modern psychologists stress the importance of the kind of learning that is primarily an active process of problem solving, although the terms used for problem solving, or goal-oriented behavior, are confusingly varied (see *The Psychology of Learning* [66, chap. vii]). Much research on learning has been interpreted as implying that the learner modifies his behavior in order to cope more adequately, in his own view, with a situation that concerns him. "Responses are selected, eliminated, organized, and stabilized in terms of their relevance to the learner's goal." (66, p. 271) It is the learner's perception of these relevancies that is crucial (see Syngg and Combs [74]). The existence of information that one person considers pertinent to a problem another person is facing will not necessarily affect the latter's behavior. He himself must see the significance. Cartwright, in an article describing the importance of group support and identification for change in behavior, states: "Information relating to the need for change, plans for change, and the consequences of change must be shared by the relevant people in the group." (10, p. 390)

11. A doctoral study completed at Teachers College by Davis (30) summarizes the answers given by practicing school people to the question: "Why is it that administrators and teachers in local school systems find it so difficult to use the results of fundamental research studies in solving their daily professional problems?" Davis concludes that research results would more quickly change practice if those whose practices are to be affected were involved in the research.

12. Foshay, Wann, and associates (39) report in some detail the reactions of teachers in a curriculum improvement program that was designed as action research. The teachers, who had all had professional training in education, commented frequently on the fact that action research enabled them to see the relationship between their own problems and the evidence they obtained in testing their action hypotheses.

13. Lippitt expresses an analogous point of view: "In the physical sciences new discoveries are absorbed rather quickly by those eager to market new products or to improve the efficiency of expensive methods. . . . In human sciences, however, the personal and group vested interests in 'keeping on doing what we're doing' are stronger and more deeply rooted as the basis for prestige and emotional security." (52, p. 7 f.) He then gives several reasons for the strong disposition to resist changes in human relations practices.

14. This reference to college entrance is only one of the observations made by Redefer (67) in 1952. It was, however, the only conclusion stressed in Fine's summary of the Redefer study, which appeared in the June 1, 1952 issue of *The New York Times*.

15. See L. S. Waskin, "The Michigan Secondary-School–College Agreement," *The Bulletin of the National Association of Secondary-School Principals*, 33:49-64, January 1949; and Johnson (46).

16. Moses (64) has written an interesting article describing some statistical methods appropriate for non-normal popula-

tions. These methods are rarely used in educational research, and they assume random sampling.

17. Redefer's investigation (67) into the consequences of the Eight Year Study—eight years later—involved visits to many of the communities that had experimented with promising curriculum innovations at the high school level ten or fifteen years ago. He concludes that few traces of these innovations are observable now and believes that the most important single reason for failure was the lack of genuine community involvement in the change process.

18. In this connection, the reader might be interested in the attempt by Benne, Axtelle, Smith, and Raup (5) to make democracy practically synonymous with the method of science as applied to human relations problems. Whittaker Chambers (14), on the other hand, equates the scientific method with communism. He argues that we must put our trust in God, not in human intelligence or experimentation. The dichotomy seems unrealistically sharp.

CHAPTER II

The Action Research Process*

In the preceding chapter action research in education was contrasted in several respects with traditional research. This chapter is an elaboration of the process of what might be called empirical action research.[1] What are the things school people do who are trying to test in action, as scientifically as possible, practices that give promise of improving education?

The following description of the action research process is based in part on a memorandum prepared with the help of Gordon N. Mackenzie and a group of Denver, Colorado, high school principals and curriculum coordinators who were cooperating with the Horace Mann-Lincoln Institute of School Experimentation in a series of studies undertaken to improve instructional leadership.[2] The illustrations used in this chapter therefore involve the decisions and actions of principals and supervisors. In Chapter III the action research process is further illustrated by two studies, one of which describes classroom experimentation by teachers.

* This chapter is an expansion of some ideas presented in "Curriculum Development through Action Research," *Educational Leadership*, 7:147-153, December 1949.

Decisions and Prediction of Consequences

Administrators and supervisors are constantly making decisions and acting on the basis of what they believe the consequences of these decisions will be. A principal, for example, may believe that appointing teachers to the chairmanship of committees (action) will result in better committee work (goal) than the choice of chairmen by the committees themselves. Sometimes it is discovered, often accidentally and much later, that the expected consequences actually do not follow. The longer a practice has been engaged in, the harder it is to see its limitations and to change. One reason for this is the tendency to perceive the expected consequences even though they are not there. Even more commonly, preconceptions about results make the perception of actual consequences so selective that concomitant and contradictory effects are ignored. Action research is one method of trying consciously to find out whether or not certain activities actually do lead to the results that were anticipated.

Probably the most important characteristic that differentiates action research from more casual inquiry is that evidence is systematically sought, recorded, and interpreted. This is done to find out more definitely just what the problem is as well as to learn what happens when certain procedures are used to deal with it. Every kind of research involves accumulating and interpreting evidence, but action research focuses on evidence that helps answer the question, Did a particular action result in the desirable consequences that were anticipated? Those conducting the research try to determine, as objectively as possible, whether the methods used to ameliorate a difficult situation actually bring about improvement. They are also interested in finding out whether other, perhaps undesirable, consequences accompany the expected results.

The Action Hypothesis

In an action research study it is common to hypothesize, or predict, that certain desired results will follow from what appear to be better practices. Here are three examples of such hypotheses, which grew out of a personal concern some status leaders felt about the quality of teacher committee work:

1. Curriculum committees made up of volunteers will be more productive than curriculum committees constituted by appointment.
2. Committee study and practice of group process will lead to increased productivity.
3. Scheduling meetings during school time will increase productivity of committees.

These three action hypotheses were not formulated merely to satisfy curiosity about what might be done to increase productivity. The basic motivation for the action research was a common, personal problem of a group of principals and curriculum coordinators. They wanted to do a better job in an area in which their inadequacy bothered them. Teachers and administrators were spending an increasing amount of time in committee work. There were frequent complaints that many of these committees did not get much done. The principals and coordinators wanted to do what they could to improve the situation.

Nature of the Hypothesis

Each of the three action research hypotheses reproduced above has two aspects. Each implies, first, a desirable goal: increased committee productivity; and second, a procedure, or action, for achieving the goal: arranging for volunteer committees, study and practice of group process, scheduling meetings on school time.

The goal made explicit in these hypotheses is only a partial goal. One of the difficulties with many actions is that the goals in view are limited. Whatever is done to achieve a specific end may actually interfere with a more comprehensive and possibly more important purpose. For example, certain steps taken to increase committee productivity, narrowly defined, might make members so anxious about their committee work or induce them to devote so much time to it that they would neglect other significant professional activities.

The difficulty of keeping in mind the great variety of purposes involved in such a complex activity as school teaching or supervision or administration is troublesome to everyone who seriously tries to do something about practical problems. Engaging in action research as a method of improving educational practices does not avoid the necessity for giving explicit attention to the interrelatedness and relativity of goals. In the more traditional kind of educational inquiry attempts are frequently made to control the experimental situation so that complexities of this sort are ruled out.[3] This practice is comforting to the investigator, but commonly results in the testing of hypotheses that bear little relation to those teachers must test in order to make better decisions about their own practices. To accumulate data, for example, that relate to a hypothesis about the way children learn to read "apart from the role of social pressure to read" may result in findings appropriate to the defined situation, but this situation does not exist in reality.

Practicing school people must, of course, deal most of the time with real situations. Because action research is conducted in an actual school environment, the investigators are almost forced to recognize that numerous goals and purposes are involved. If the action research is cooperative, the diversity of interests and concerns of the various members of the group gives added assurance that more comprehensive goals will not be lost sight of in attempts to do something concrete about a particular problem.

Although school activities should not be planned to achieve narowly defined goals, the necessity remains, in action research, for eventually formulating a delimited hypothesis as carefully and precisely as possible. When the statement of this hypothesis indicates a goal and a method or methods of achieving it, an important initial step has been taken. Identification of problems is sometimes made easier by first phrasing them as questions. For research purposes it is helpful to rephrase these questions later to make explicit a procedure, or action, and a goal.

Here are four questions raised by a group that was just starting to conduct research in order to improve the educational leadership of its members:

> What leadership techniques are best in working with teachers?
> How can teacher planning meetings be made more successful?
> How can a principal work most effectively with teachers?
> What are the factors that create job satisfaction?

Questions like these imply a desire for answers; they do not, however, serve as suggestions for experimentation that will test plausible answers. They indicate the need for research, but they do not, in their present form, give much help in designing a study that will result in a sounder basis for decisions and actions. Before action research could be undertaken in the broad area covered by the first question, for example, it would be necessary to describe leadership procedures in rather specific terms and then predict the consequences of practicing them. If the procedures seemed promising to the investigators, they would be put into practice, and data would be gathered to determine whether or not and to what degree the expected results were obtained.

Sources of the Hypothesis

It is always important to consider the sources of the action hypotheses formulated by a group attempting to use research as a method of improving its decisions and actions. Obviously, the hypotheses do not come from the air. Usually they represent specific applications of a more or less consciously formulated theory or system of beliefs. In this case, for example, the more inclusive theory about committee activity was one that viewed production as closely related to motivation. Although this conviction, or element of theory, was not made explicit, it served as one source of the action hypotheses that members of the group decided to test. Other sources were materials they had read and ideas they had picked up from one another in discussion. Reports of traditional research investigations frequently are fruitful sources of hypotheses to test in actual school situations.

One mark of sophistication in scientific problem solving is an awareness of theory and a disposition to use the evidence from the testing of action hypotheses to build theory. This is a difficult task. Careful theorizing is probably only slightly less common in action research than it is in traditional research. Although professional researchers are inclined to emphasize theory when their attention is called specifically to it, this emphasis is not at all evident in most of their research reports.

An Illustrative Action Research

The following actual hypothesis, one of many that might be formulated in connection with the question, "What leadership techniques are best in working with teachers?" was phrased in a way that would make a test possible:

> Curriculum committees made up of volunteers [action] will be more productive [goal] than curriculum committees constituted by appointment [alternative action].

The research process, in the broad sense, had of course been under way some time before this hypothesis was formulated. The process started when members of the group expressed their personal concern about the general problem of improving leadership. There was a great deal of discussion and reading as attempts were made to identify and make use of ideas that various authors had developed or certain members of the group had heard about or tried out. As interest in the improvement of leadership became more specific, it became clear that one area in which leadership was exercised extensively was teacher committee work. There again was considerable discussion and reading to find out what members of the group, as well as "experts" who had written on teacher committee activity, had to say about how best to facilitate this kind of work.

During this stage of the research process several action hypotheses or hunches were considered. One was that committee productivity would be improved if the principal, prior to appointing a committee, interviewed several prospective members to try to determine their interest in the committee's task. The proposal was explored rather thoroughly in discussion; this process amounted to trying it out in imagination. The tentative conclusion reached was that the plan was not particularly promising, because the same results might be achieved with less trouble by calling for committee volunteers.

Another action hypothesis considered was to appoint the chairmen of various committees and allow them to fill out the committee rosters. This hypothesis also was rejected, after some discussion, because too little was known about the procedure that might be followed by these chairmen. It was thought, for example, that they might attempt to appoint their friends to the committee; the selection would then be based primarily on social compatibility.

These initial research activities were not substantially

different from those in which most individuals or groups engage when they meet to discuss ways and means of solving a particular problem. The more nearly unique aspects of action research began to emerge with the formulation of a hypothesis to be tested in action and a prediction of consequences. There was a real difference of opinion within the group regarding the relative productivity of volunteer committees and committees constituted by "intelligent" appointment. The reading and discussion in which the group engaged sometimes did not make clear what was meant by *appointing* and *volunteering*. There seemed to be almost no evidence to support the arguments of proponents of either method.

After the hypothesis finally selected for testing had been formulated, the group realized that its big job would be to develop ways and means of measuring productivity. In order to conduct an investigation that would test the hypothesis, certain procedures had to be planned and carried out.

1. It was necessary to define what was meant by "volunteering."

This was not very difficult, although teachers often say, "If it's a voluntary meeting, we'd better go!" It was agreed that in this context *volunteering* referred to the way the committee members regarded the situation and not to any pronouncement from administrators.

2. It was necessary to define what was meant by "appointing."

There might be a vast difference in productivity between committees whose members were randomly appointed and those whose members were appointed with some consideration of individual needs and interests.

3. It was necessary to describe clearly how productivity was to be measured.

This was hard to do. Productivity has many dimensions.

It may refer to the dispatch with which a specific job is accomplished. A broader conception implies improvement in group work methods, which will enable the committee to carry out its next job more efficiently. An even more comprehensive conception of productivity would take into consideration the increased security and effectiveness of individual members of the committees.[4] This particular group, considering productivity rather narrowly, decided that the work a committee did was to be measured by the following:

   a. The number of action decisions reached per unit of time. (The way these action decisions are made is also important. Are they all suggested by the status leader? Do they represent consensus? Is responsibility for actions delegated by the group?)
   b. The per cent of action decisions carried out.
   c. The per cent of decisions and/or actions subsequently judged to have been successful in achieving the committee's purposes.
   d. The evaluation by committee members of their own productivity.
   e. The evaluation by outsiders of the committee's productivity.

The first and second items in this operational definition of committee productivity imply observations that are objective and can be counted. An outsider could look at the records of committee meetings and at subsequent actions by the committees, tabulate the number of action decisions reached, and calculate the percentage carried out. This does not mean, of course, that such relatively objective evidence assures agreement in interpreting it. Items *c, d,* and *e* are obviously judgments and therefore subject to all the limitations of such estimates. Educational practitioners, as well as people engaged in other types of practical activities, are often forced to make decisions on the basis of evidence of this kind.

If the judgments are rendered under circumstances that give reasonable assurance that they are thoughtful, and not biased unduly by the state of the judge's health or disposition, they will provide more useful evidence than is ordinarily available.

4. It was necessary to measure the productivity of the volunteer committee and the appointed committee under circumstances that made the method of selecting members the crucial variable.

This task raised many troublesome questions. Was committee productivity influenced primarily by the way members were selected, or were other factors responsible for differences? Was increased productivity accompanied by other, perhaps undesirable, consequences? Were individuals in the two committees of comparable ability and comparably interested in the committee's tasks?

5. It was necessary to carry out these plans in a way that would make possible the accumulation of data to appraise their worth.

This aspect of action research brought to the attention of the group many of the well-known questions about the nature of evidence, its reliability, and its validity. These people were helped to recognize that reliability and validity are relative. If evidence could be collected that was *more* reliable and *more* valid than the evidence previously available for guiding decisions and evaluating actions based on these decisions, that much would be gained.

6. It was necessary to interpret these data to see if and to what degree they supported or refuted the hypothesis.

Here, too, the action researchers faced difficult and complex problems. How great must differences be if they are to have any practical significance? Statistical significance is no assurance of practical significance, although many reports of traditional research overlook this distinction. What conclusion should be reached if members of the volunteer committee felt better about what they were doing, and supported and encouraged one another, but the appointed committee accomplished specific tasks with more dispatch? Productivity is quite likely to result in greater achievement along one dimension by one group and greater achievement along another dimension by a second group.

7. It was necessary to infer from the data generalizations that would guide action in future situations. These generalizations would have to be applied and continuously tested.

The group realized that because productivity is in large measure a function of the specific situation in which any committee works, continuous testing of consequences would be needed. Action research is cyclical. The studies undertaken to guide decisions regarding the method of constituting committees revealed new problems, which in turn suggested the need for new action hypotheses to be tested.[5]

The group tried to remember that committee productivity was not the *summum bonum*. Teachers have other things to do, and the fact that a certain practice results in increased committee productivity does not necessarily mean that the practice should be encouraged. The total responsibilities of teachers must be kept in mind, and specific practices appraised in relation to some broad conception of the teacher's task.

The partial description that has just been given of one action research project may have made this method of coping with practical educational problems seem unduly formidable. However, all aspects of the process may be carried out at various levels of quality. This point is developed at greater length in Chapter IV. It is always difficult to conduct clear-cut, definitive research, and action research is no exception. Consequently, some people reject this method of dealing with educational problems. They say it is too slow, or too complicated, or too pretentious. They seem to prefer to go to the opposite extreme and act on the basis of casual evidence, which is presumed to support vaguely implied action hypotheses.[6]

Action Research and Cooperation

Nothing inherent in action research requires such inquiries to be cooperative, that is, to involve a number of people jointly in an attack on a practical problem. Quite frequently individual school people can conduct research to help them make better decisions and evaluate actions that have to do with their own teaching or administrative problems.

A teacher, for example, is worried because he does not have sufficient time to do the things he wants to do. Out of this broad problem area he differentiates a more specific aspect: the time he spends scoring the objective examinations he gives twice a week. It takes him approximately forty-five minutes to score objective examinations one mimeographed page long for his two different classes in the same subject.

The teacher formulates several action hypotheses for saving time. The source of these proposals for action may be his own experience, his reading, or conversations with other people. One hypothesis involves giving tests less frequently. This, however, conflicts with the broader goal of frequent pupil evaluation. The hypothesis that shortening the tests would save scoring time also conflicts with the same important educational goal. A third hypothesis involves making a scoring key for each test.

The action suggested by the third hypothesis is taken, and the evidence of its success is that the tests can be scored in fifteen minutes instead of forty-five minutes. Even if five minutes are allowed for making the key, this represents a substantial saving in time. The major generalization resulting from this research is relatively concrete and leads the teacher to make scoring stencils in the future.

There is no reason why this activity should not be called action research. A large percentage of the problems faced by teachers, administrators, and supervisors, however, cannot be solved unless a number of people change their views and practices. In recognition of this fact several recent texts stress the importance of cooperative work on educational problems if the problems affect a number of people.[7] One great advantage in making action research cooperative is that involvement of many people in problem identification and analysis, in hypothesizing, and in data collecting and interpreting increases the likelihood that there will be strong commitments to change behavior if the consequences of the study indicate change is warranted.

When action research is cooperative, the probability also increases that whatever actions are hypothesized will be within the realm of possibility. It is unlikely that a group of teachers who are concerned because they know too little about their pupils would hypothesize that their teaching would improve if they were to make case studies for each pupil. If the teachers had even a general idea of what was involved in a case study, they would recognize immediately that making one for each of thirty or forty or, in the high school, two hundred and fifty different pupils is far beyond the realm of reasonable expectation. The proposal would only be made by those who did not intend to carry it out.

Another reason for making action research cooperative is to provide a greater range and variety of talent at each stage of the action research process. Individual members of the group have different perceptions, experiences, and competencies, and these variations can enrich the entire research activity.

A number of socio-psychological investigations have contrasted the quality of group and individual problem solving.

The problems that were set for the individuals or groups in these studies were usually quite artificial, however. The motivation was assumed, and no action was expected to result from the problem solving. Despite these limitations, Murphy, Murphy, and Newcomb, after summarizing a considerable number of such investigations, conclude:

> From such studies the superior value of group thinking over individual thinking, when demonstrated, is clearly due in part to (1) the larger number of ways of looking at the problem; (2) the larger number of suggestions for a solution; (3) the larger number of effective criticisms of each proposed plan; (4) the patent need to accept social criticism and not be bull-headed (as subjects working alone frequently are). (65, p. 738)

Final consideration of the relative worth of individual and group proposals for dealing with practical problems must be postponed until the suggested proposal is actually put into effect and tested. There is no doubt that particular individuals in most working groups, because of their background and intelligence, are able orally or in writing to propose what appear to be excellent solutions to practical problems. When these solutions are considered in the abstract, against certain criteria of logic, they may seem to be better than those favored by the group as a whole. The difficulty is that the effectiveness of any action is conditioned by the background, insight, and ability of the people who must carry it out. In a sense this means that the action recommended by a group probably represents the best that the members, at the time, are able to do.

When a group of educational practitioners identifies a problem of sufficient concern to make each person feel that something must be done about it, many kinds of competency and special talent may be required. There are times when the group will want to confer with, or use as a consultant, an individual outside the group who can give special help. Frequently assistance is needed from someone who can provide help with the research process itself.[8]

Another important consequence of cooperative research is that the co-workers constitute a group that provides considerable support to individuals for risking change. Any kind of experimentation involves risk.[9] If the consequences could be guaranteed, no research would be needed. When these risks become visible, the fact that "there are several of us who are trying this out" is invariably supporting. Evans [10] and the people he worked with in Battle Creek to develop a tenth-grade general education program concluded that building a cooperative group for action research was so important that "it seems hardly possible to us for any reconstruction of the high school program to proceed very far unless teachers learn to work closely together in problem-centered groups." (37, p. 473)

The strong feeling of group identification that frequently results from cooperative action research or any other well-motivated group activity is not, however, an unmixed blessing. Unless precautions are taken, the research group may become something of a pedagogical island in a generally hostile faculty environment. For a group to develop the kind of spirit that supports cooperative work, and at the same time to have a judicious and perceptive attitude toward staff morale, requires a nice balance among values.[11]

A final reason for making action research cooperative, especially in connection with curriculum improvement, is that cooperation tends to prevent those involved from feeling that they are being manipulated or coerced. When a number of teachers work together to identify specific problems for attack, use their experience to hypothesize actions that give promise of ameliorating a difficult situation, and together work through all the other phases of action research, it is unlikely that anyone will feel he is being experimented on without his consent.

These references to the importance of cooperative action research call attention, at least by implication, to some sociological as well as psychological factors that influence changes in behavior. Redefer (67), as a result of his inquiry into the consequences of the Eight Year Study, eight years later, was confident that the great omission in that important experiment in secondary education was its neglect of the sociological factors involved in learning. Too many of the people whose support was essential to maintaining the experimental programs had no part in planning or developing or evaluating them.

Conclusion

This chapter has analyzed a kind of research that is intended to result in improved practices. The reader already has recognized that this analysis is in many respects similar to Dewey's 1916 statement (31) about the nature of thinking, which he revised in 1933.[12] The chief differences are the greater emphasis upon evidence, upon the *action* hypothesis, and upon the importance of *cooperative* research when a number of people are concerned about a problem and will be affected by whatever is done to solve it.

The significant elements of a design for action research are:

1. The identification of a problem area about which an individual or a group is sufficiently concerned to want to take some action.
2. The selection of a specific problem and the formulation of a hypothesis or prediction that implies a goal and a procedure for reaching it. This specific goal must be viewed in relation to the total situation.
3. The careful recording of actions taken and the accumulation of evidence to determine the degree to which the goal has been achieved.

4. The inference from this evidence of generalizations regarding the relation between the actions and the desired goal.
5. The continuous retesting of these generalizations in action situations.

If the problem under attack is one of concern to many people, or if it is likely that the experiment will affect many people, the action research should involve these people. It then becomes *cooperative* action research.

The best way to learn how to engage in action research is to try it. After commenting on the difficulty they had with the research function, the teachers working with Evans write: "But we feel that the only way we can become more competent in classroom research is to *do* classroom research, even though we may lack many needed skills and insights." (37, p. 472)

Reading about what others have done provides only limited help. One of the excellent incidental effects of conducting action research is that the people involved come to some disturbing conclusions about their tendency to generalize without evidence. A particular action research study may be criticized because it results in evidence of limited reliability and validity, but the very insistence on trying to get some evidence is a sign of increasing maturity in problem solving.

NOTES TO

CHAPTER II

1. Chein, Cook, and Harding (15) identify four varieties of action research but make it clear that there are no sharp lines of demarcation between them. They write about *diagnostic* action research, which is designed to lead to action; *participant* action research, which emphasizes that the people who are to take action must be involved in the research process from the beginning; *empirical* action research, which involves doing something and keeping a record of what is done and what happens; and *experimental* action research, which is controlled research on the relative effectiveness of various action techniques. These authors point out that of the four kinds of action research, the experimental seems to have the greatest value for the advancement of scientific knowledge because, under favorable circumstances, it can provide a definitive test of specific hypotheses. The authors also say that it is the most difficult form of action research to carry on successfully.

2. For a report of these studies see Mackenzie, Corey, and associates (57).

3. Caswell (11), in a thoughtful article dealing with research in the curriculum field, calls attention to limitations of experimentation that is removed from real situations. He believes that the action research approach is "highly encouraging" but expresses apprehension lest this type of inquiry should place insufficient emphasis on generalization.

4. An analysis of the total task of a group can be approached in several ways, as Benne and Sheats (4) suggest. The actual

preparation of a resource unit in the social studies area might be the central task. Learning how to work together more effectively, so that another resource unit developed later will be a better one, is a conception of task at the level of process. Providing an atmosphere in which individuals can gain deeper insight into themselves and achieve a better-integrated total personality represents still a different level of task analysis.

5. Eight action research studies were analyzed by Lippitt and Radke (53) in order to identify the "major points of procedure." These authors call attention to the "spiral" nature of action research and suggest that communicating the results of inquiry to other groups, orally or in written form, can be a final step or, more likely, a new first step.

6. The method of science has so far had relatively little influence on the way practitioners, not only in education but in other fields, attack their day-to-day problems. In 1947 Lundberg, a sociologist especially interested in the application of the scientific method to social problems, said:

> I am aware that the scientific mode of thought is very recent in human history, that it is practiced by only a very small percentage of our own generation and that it is uncongenial to a large number of otherwise admirable people. (56, p. 13)

Dewey had said almost the same thing thirty years earlier and had cited some reasons that appeared significant to him:

> The experimental method is new as a scientific resource—as a systematized means of making knowledge, though as old as life as a practical device. Hence it is not surprising that men have not recognized its full scope. For the most part, its significance is regarded as belonging to certain technical and merely physical matters. It will doubtless take a long time to secure the perception that it holds equally as to the forming and testing of ideas in social and moral matters. Men still want the crutch of dogma, of beliefs fixed by authority, to relieve them of the trouble of thinking and the responsibility of directing their activity by thought. . . . But every advance in the influence of the experimental method is sure to aid in outlawing the literary, dialectic and authoritative methods of forming beliefs which have governed the schools of the past, and to transfer their prestige to

methods which will procure an active concern with things and persons, directed by aims of increasing temporal reach and deploying greater range of things in space. (31, p. 394 f.)

7. There has been a great increase in teacher participation in curriculum improvement, and this participation has usually taken the form of group activity. Curriculum workers soon learned that a great deal of skill is necessary if groups are to be productive. The following authors give attention to the importance of efficient methods of group work in cooperative curriculum development: Benne and Muntyan (3), Campbell (9), Koopman, Miel, and Misner (48), Miel (61), and Yauch (80). One of the best recent statements of the implications of this problem for social research in general is by Mann (59).

8. Lawler's study (50) and the dissertation by Troyer (76) stress the difference between resource people who direct and tell and those who work with a group. Jahoda, Deutsch, and Cook (45) emphasize the necessity in action research for close collaboration between the research specialist and field groups.

9. The article by Foshay and Hall (38) summarizes the meaning and significance that cooperative classroom experimentation had for a group of curriculum workers. These people were well aware of the risks taken in action research.

10. This report by Evans and his associates (37) is a rather complete description of one attempt to develop a "new" curriculum by the method of action research.

11. In connection with morale and curricular experimentation, the group working with Evans states: "Every effort is made to prevent the new development from becoming an 'island' in the total program. Keeping the faculty informed concerning development is essential. Whenever possible, various members of the staff are brought in as consultants. Individual members of the cooperating group inform their colleagues about this work in progress whenever occasion offers an opportunity." (37, p. 424)

12. In *How We Think* Dewey describes a series of steps that he believes to be involved in reflective thinking. The ultimate consequence of reflective thinking, according to Dewey, is coming to some conclusion or reaching some generalization. In connection with his discussion of "Inference in testing," Dewey says: "Suggested inferences are tested in *thought* to see whether different elements in the suggestion are coherent with one another. They are also tested, after one has been adopted, by *action* to see whether the consequences that are anticipated in *thought* occur in *fact*." (32, p. 97) He goes on to say: "The two methods do not differ, however, in kind. Testing in thought for consistency involves acting in *imagination*. The other mode carries the imagined act out overtly." (32, p. 98) Dewey identifies these five phases, or aspects, of reflective thought: suggestion, intellectualization, hypothesizing, reasoning, and testing the hypothesis by action. He then says: "The concluding stage is some kind of testing by overt action to give *experimental corroboration,* or *verification,* of the conjectural idea." (32, p. 113 f.) Dewey makes it clear that he does not believe that the sequence of the five phases is fixed.

CHAPTER III

Two Action Research Studies

In *this chapter two articles are reprinted which illustrate how practical school people have improved their decisions and actions by attacking their problems more scientifically. These action research studies are not offered as perfect illustrations of what might be done to solve concrete, practical problems by engaging in research. They do indicate, however, that supervisors and teachers, not particularly interested in research in the abstract, found the research method an appropriate and rewarding way of coping with their difficulties. The first study was undertaken to improve teacher planning meetings, and illustrates action research on a supervisory problem. The second study was conducted by a group of high school teachers to improve their instruction in American history.*

ACTION RESEARCH TO IMPROVE TEACHER PLANNING MEETINGS[*]

MARY NEEL SMITH

For several years the Gove Junior High School staff has been engaged in programs of curriculum development and instructional improvement. Much of the work has been done through co-operative teacher planning sessions, which are under the general leadership of the co-ordinator of instruction. Since this planning, with the exception of the "case conferences," is done on school time, it is considered a regular part of the teachers' load.

The teachers involved in the planning meetings may be those who teach the same subjects, those who teach a particular half-grade level of a subject, or those who teach different subjects to the same child or group of children. The number of teachers involved in any one planning group varies from two to nine. The meetings are called at the request of the co-ordinator of instruction, or the elected chairman of the group, or some other group member. We have avoided scheduling meetings at regular intervals but have held them whenever they were thought to be necessary.

While these meetings accomplished some of the purposes for which they were established, they were not completely satisfactory. Consequently, we decided to work rather directly for their improvement. The general procedure employed as we tried to make the teacher planning meetings

[*] This study was reported by Mary Neel Smith in *The School Review*, 60:142-150, March 1952. It was one of a number of similar investigations resulting from cooperation between secondary school principals and co-ordinators from Denver, Colorado, and research consultants from the Horace Mann-Lincoln Institute of School Experimentation. The article is reprinted by permission of the author and *The School Review*.

more effective might be called "operational research" or "action research." It involved, first, a study of the total teacher planning situation, the collecting of as much evidence as possible to indicate what the difficulties might be. We then selected one or more specific problems to work on intensively. Our next step was to formulate action hypotheses that seemed to give promise of eliminating or reducing the seriousness of the problem. These actions were then carried out, and we not only kept a record of what was done but also tried to get as much evidence as possible regarding the consequences of the changes in practices related to teacher planning meetings. Finally, from this evidence we drew generalizations to provide further guides to our activities.

We would not like to imply that these steps were necessarily taken seriatim. It should be emphasized, too, that the action-research process is continuous. For example, evidence on the consequences of our changed activities almost always called attention to new problems and new difficulties which could best be understood and coped with by engaging in another operational-research project.

The Problems

Difficulties Encountered

The difficulties that seemed to keep the teacher planning meetings from being maximally successful are listed below, with suggestions of the kind of evidence that caused us to feel as we did.

1. A general impression that many of the meetings were not worth while.

Our evidence for this feeling, though not objective, was of several types. There frequently had been verbal resistance to the meetings. During some of the meetings, activities engaged in by the teachers, such as making out report cards or checking papers, implied that at least a substantial minority of the group were not too concerned with what was going on. Now and then a scheduled meeting would be canceled by the group chairman because of lack of clarity as to its purpose.

2. Lack of a feeling of responsibility for the success of meetings by the members of the group.

Participation in the meetings was limited to a few people. Proposals for action were frequently made. When proposals were made, there seemed to be little interest in volunteering to do the interim work that might be required to carry out the action.

3. Assumption of too much responsibility by the status leader—the co-ordinator of instruction.

The co-ordinator felt strongly that she took responsibility for too many of the activities. She felt, too, that this almost inevitably resulted in the feeling on the part of the other members of the group that "this is the co-ordinator's meeting" rather than "this is our meeting."

4. Lack of assurance that decisions made by the group would be carried out.

Our evidence on this point was based, in part, upon casual conversations here and there. Our records of meetings, though incomplete, also indicated that many decisions for action did not result in any action.

5. General lack of attention to better methods of group work in the planning meetings.

The evidence for this was again subjective, but persuasive. Almost never did any member of the group suggest a better method of working than the one that had become habitual.

Evidence from Interviews with the Principal

We realized that we should have better evidence on the attitudes of the teachers toward these planning meetings and the reasons for their attitudes. Consequently, the principal, during the course of her regular interviews with the teachers, asked these questions, which she and the co-ordinator had formulated:

> What do you think of the teacher planning meetings?
>
> In what ways have the meetings been helpful?
>
> What changes might be effected in order to make them most helpful?
>
> Do you have an opportunity to get at problems that are meaningful to you? Why? Why not?
>
> What responsibility have you personally taken for the success of these meetings?
>
> What suggestions for improvement have you?

The teachers were not particularly critical of the meetings. They said the meetings were helpful as occasions for discussing scope and sequence of instruction, as well as materials and techniques related to the units they were teaching. Most of the teachers indicated that they had not taken much responsibility, that there did not seem to them to be anything much that they could do. One of them said, "The co-ordinator is the status leader, and she takes the responsibility."

These comments suggested that it would be a good idea to explore with the planning group the meaning of "taking responsibility." Most of the teachers did not seem to be aware, for example, that participation in discussion is a form of responsibility acceptance. At least one teacher explicitly, and others implicitly, seemed to believe that the success of the meeting was the status leader's responsibility.

Evidence from Evaluation Sheets

One method of judging the effectiveness of the meetings was to ask the teachers to check a list of ten statements as being "Most favorable or most satisfactory," "Somewhat favorable or somewhat satisfactory," or "Least favorable or unsatisfactory." The rating sheets were filled out anonymously. The two items which had the lowest average score and seemed to be related to the general problem of the sharing of responsibility for the success of co-operative planning meetings were: "One or two people seemed to dominate," and "I volunteered to do work for the group." It is interesting to find that the group indicated its realization that sometimes one or two persons were doing more than their share.

The teachers were also asked to check items on a list of suggestions for improving the meetings for the coming semester. The following suggestions were most frequently checked:

    Continue to plan agenda co-operatively.

    Keep track of the decisions we make to see whether we do anything about them.

    Take more responsibility as individuals for contributing to the success of our meetings by expressing opinions, raising questions, etc.

Action Hypotheses

In order to make a frontal attack on some of these problems, we formulated two hypotheses that we felt were supported by educational and psychological theory. These hypotheses are presented below.

Hypothesis 1

The limiting by the status leader of her comments in teacher planning meetings to (a) clarifying the statements of others, (b) reflecting the feelings of the group members, (c) raising questions, (d) calling attention to resources that might be used by the group, and (e) trying to sensitize the group to some elements of better group-work methods, will result in the assumption by its members of greater responsibility for the success of the group's activity.

This action, which involved a decided change in the behavior of the co-ordinator of instruction, was undertaken because of the conviction that it would bear directly on Problems 2, 3, and 5 listed above.

Hypothesis 2

If (*a*) the agenda of the teacher planning meetings are co-operatively planned, (*b*) records of decisions are kept and a check is made to see whether anything is done about them, and (*c*) each individual is encouraged to assume responsibility, the teacher planning meetings will seem more worth while to the group members.

These actions seem directly related to Problems 1 and 4 listed above and resulted from the written and anonymous evaluations made by the teachers.

A number of problems are faced in conducting action research of the sort that we undertook. One of the most difficult is to get evidence of substantial reliability and validity which will show whether the actions undertaken resulted in the anticipated consequences. There are all degrees of quality of evidence. We decided to get the best evidence we could under the circumstances and, as we went along, to try to get better evidence. We tried not to be discouraged if at first our research data seemed fallible, for we were at least getting *some* evidence in areas in which we heretofore had acted on the basis of subjective impressions only.

We selected one of the teacher planning groups for concentrated investigation. This group was made up of six teachers who had not worked together previously as a planning group. All were new in the grade and area in which they were teaching, and there seemed to be no visible leadership within the group. Consequently, there was great dependence upon the status leader.

Testing Hypothesis 1

We began to test Hypothesis 1 during September, 1949. We procured evidence (1) by keeping a record in the form of minutes of the group meetings; (2) by studying interviews held with each member of the group by the school principal; (3) by using an evaluation questionnaire at the end of the first, second, and third semesters.

Inasmuch as the first hypothesis involved getting evidence of a change in responsibility acceptance, we defined "responsibility" as follows:

1. Participating orally in the meeting.
2. Making suggestions for the agenda.
3. Making proposals for action.
4. Voluntarily accepting responsibility for a job to be done for the group.
5. Completing the job accepted.

With respect to each of these elements we could get rather objective evidence of any growth that took place. The group co-operatively developed a "Meeting Record Form," which helped us keep track of the co-operatively planned agenda, any action decisions made, and participation by individuals. Building this form was a good way for all of us to reach a better understanding of democratic group process and its implications for improving meetings generally. As we used this first form, we had difficulty in recording the "Proposals for Action" in such a way that looking at them afterward made their meaning clear. Consequently, a revised form was used during the third semester. We now are giving even more attention to the importance of records of meetings.

Evidence from the Minutes

The extent to which there was improvement in responsibility acceptance over a three-semester period is indicated in Table 1. These data relate directly to Hypothesis 1 and are derived from examination of the minutes of the meetings. There was considerable evidence that the consistent attempt on the part of the co-ordinator to limit her participation during most of each meeting to the kinds outlined in Hypothesis 1 did result in more acceptance of responsibility on the part of the other teachers. For example, during the first semester of 1949–50 there were 99 instances of participation, which increased to 171 during the second semester, and to 164 in the third semester with one less teacher involved. There was no increase in the frequency with which agenda items were suggested. In respect to proposals for action, there was an appreciable increase in the second semester over the first, and in the third over the second. This also was true for the frequency with which members of the group volunteered to do jobs and the frequency with which they completed the jobs undertaken.

Evidence from the Evaluation Questionnaire

Four of the six teachers in the group indicated that they felt we frequently carried out our decision to take responsibility as individuals for the success of the meeting. This evaluation tends to show that the members of the group were aware of their assumption of greater responsibility. Five of the six indicated their opinion that, so far as actual participation went, everyone assumed responsibility for the success of the meetings. The comments made on the February, 1950, and June, 1950, evaluation sheets showed a growth in concern for improving our ways of working.

During the third semester (1950–51) the group appointed a subcommittee of two of its own members and the co-

TABLE 1

Frequency with Which Six Teachers in Experimental Group Accepted Responsibility in Meetings Held Over Three-Semester Period *

Teacher and Semester †	Participation	Agenda Suggestions	Proposals for Action	Volunteering for Jobs	Completing Jobs
Teacher A:					
First semester	8	2	0	0	0
Second semester	27	0	3	0	0
Third semester	11	2	0	5	4
Teacher B:					
First semester	19	1	1	0	0
Second semester	42	0	3	0	0
Third semester	32	2	14	7	7
Teacher C:					
First semester	28	3	5	3	3
Second semester	36	9	12	3	3
Third semester	40	7	11	5	4
Teacher D:					
First semester	13	1	1	1	2
Second semester	21	0	3	3	6
Third semester	34	0	5	9	5
Teacher E:					
First semester	17	1	1	3	2
Second semester	24	0	3	9	3
Third semester ‡	..	..	..	..	..
Teacher F:					
First semester	14	4	1	1	1
Second semester	21	0	0	6	6
Third semester	47	0	0	9	9
Total:					
First semester	99	12	9	8	8
Second semester	171	9	24	21	18
Third semester	164	11	30	35	29

* These records covered different numbers of meetings during the first, the second, and the third semesters. The data are reported as if nine meetings had been recorded each semester. We recognize the dangers in this type of extrapolation.

† The first semester ran from September, 1949, to January, 1950; the second, from February to June, 1950; the third, from September, 1950, to January, 1951.

‡ Teacher E was in military service in the third semester.

ordinator to study evaluation instruments and recommend a form to be used by the group. The subcommittee met three times and carried out the responsibility assumed. This represents the largest interim job undertaken by members of the group and a willingness on the part of two members to do a job for the benefit of the six.

Testing Hypothesis 2

We began to test the second hypothesis at the start of the second semester (February, 1950). Evidence was procured in the following ways: (1) by keeping a record in the form of minutes of the meeting (this was done by a member selected by the group on a form developed co-operatively); (2) by keeping a record of process, that is, the observer's record (the building co-ordinator kept this record); (3) by using a questionnaire at the end of the first, second, and third semesters.

Planning Agenda Co-operatively

If the purpose of teacher planning meetings is to deal with problems significant to the group involved, the value of planning the agenda co-operatively cannot be overstressed. Only as a proposed agenda is reacted to by members of the group or as items for the agenda are suggested by members of the group can there be certainty that problems meaningful to all are considered.

The observer's records with respect to our attempts to plan the agenda co-operatively indicated that the chairman of the group (Teacher C) assumed the greatest responsibility, perhaps understandably so. However, two other persons made suggestions in the third semester compared with none other in the second. As has been stated, Table 1 indicates no increase in the frequency with which agenda items were suggested. The first semester seems to have had greatest participation in agenda-building with all six members of the group suggesting items for the agenda.

The group itself registered a divided opinion in this area on the evaluation questionnaire of February, 1951. Three members indicated that they felt we frequently carried out our decision to plan the agenda co-operatively, and three indicated that we did so some of the time. The fact that no meeting was held unless a poll of the members of the group showed that they felt a need for it might represent a degree of co-operative planning not indicated in the observer's record of actual meetings. Be that as it may, we seem to have made least progress in the area of co-operative agenda planning.

Checking to See Whether We Carried through Decisions

Table 1 shows that the number of proposals for action increased greatly during the second and the third semesters —an indication that the group members were assuming more and more responsibility for the success of the meetings. The minutes and the observer's notes made it clear that actions decided on were carried out. The fact that the chairman checked on decisions made at the previous meeting helped to sensitize the group to the importance of following through. In the February, 1951, evaluation, five of the six teachers felt that we frequently carried out our resolution to keep track of our decisions and to see whether we took action on them, and one thought that we sometimes did.

Feeling of Worth-whileness of Meetings

On the written evaluation in February, 1951, five teachers out of six indicated that they felt the meetings during the third semester were worth while; the sixth member indicated that the meetings were *very* worth while. The records of the meetings are evidence of a relationship between this feeling and the actions inherent in Hypothesis 2.

One bit of concrete evidence of a feeling of the worthwhileness of this kind of meeting was the group's acceptance of one member's suggestion to plan a series of demonstration lessons to be held on two consecutive mornings in November, followed by a half-day (meetings are usually forty-five minutes long) meeting on Friday. The plan was entirely group-made. The co-ordinator served only as facilitator, scheduling the meetings, requesting substitute teachers, and so on. Following this half-day planning meeting, we used a post-meeting evaluation form. Two teachers thought the session "very satisfactory," and four rated it "satisfactory."

Interim and Final Evaluation

Three times during this study the six teachers involved were asked to respond to the meeting evaluation sheet which was used originally. The first response might indicate the "bench mark," or the place at which we began; the second response, an evaluation at the halfway point; and the third response, the final evaluation of the three-semester effort. These reactions are summarized in Table 2.

The data in this table indicate less improvement in general feelings about the meeting than we had hoped for. We were encouraged by the responses to Items 2, 5, 6, 7, and 10. The implication is that factors had been at work to draw the individuals in the working group closer together. Responses to Item 9 are interesting because the actual records of the meetings over the three-semester period showed that there was an increase in the frequency of volunteering for jobs. The contradiction of opinion by factual evidence has led us to interpret with caution data derived from subjective recollections.

TABLE 2

Weighted Reactions of Experimental Group to Statements about Teacher Planning Meetings

Statement	Weighted Response* February 1950	June 1950	February 1951
1. I felt that my ideas counted	2.5	2.8	2.3
2. We all seemed to assume responsibility for the success of the meeting	2.7	2.7	2.8
3. I believe my time was wasted	3.0	2.8	2.5
4. We discussed things that were not important to me	2.5	2.3	2.5
5. One or two people seemed to dominate	2.0	2.5	2.5
6. I felt that I was an active member of the group	2.5	3.0	2.8
7. I tended to withdraw from the group	2.3	2.3	2.7
8. We had the impression that we were accomplishing the things we set out to do	2.8	2.7	2.5
9. I volunteered to do work for the group	2.5	2.4	2.0
10. We carried out our decisions	2.5	2.5	2.7

* The following values were given the responses: most favorable or most satisfactory, 3; somewhat favorable or somewhat satisfactory, 2; and least favorable or unsatisfactory, 1.

Generalizations and Conclusions

We believe that the way we went about trying to improve our teacher planning meetings was most helpful. We defined our problems more carefully than we had before. Our emphasis upon trying to get evidence describing the consequences of our actions helped us realize how much of what we ordinarily do is based on vague, subjective impressions. In addition to these general conclusions, our data seem to support the following, more specific generalizations.

1. This group assumed more responsibility for the success of its meetings when the status leader provided maximum opportunity for growth by limiting her own participation and by helping the group become sensitive to better ways of working.
2. Not only did the quantity of responsibility assumed by group members increase, but the quality of the responsibility that was assumed improved noticeably. Increased participation per se was one of the earliest stages in the assumption of responsibility. Proposals for action and the doing of interim work for the group were later stages and were probably indicative of greater group maturity.
3. The use of written evaluation sheets to "get at" ideas for improving meetings is a good method for developing a group's concern about its own ways of working and its achievements. The reporting of summaries of such sheets to the group usually led to discussions concerning better ways of working.
4. Checking to see whether anything has been done about decisions made at previous meetings is another way of sensitizing the group to the importance of "carrying through" on decisions. This implies a functional use of the record of the previous meeting.
5. Intensive work with one teacher group can affect many other planning groups within the school, since the individuals are also members of other groups. In this situation, concern for planning agenda co-operatively, for assuming responsibility for the success of meetings, and for keeping track of decisions has spread to other groups through members of the experimental group and the co-ordinator.
6. The records of the meetings imply greater growth in improved ways of working than do the evaluation sheets.

7. Ways of helping groups become sensitive to more effective methods of working need to be carefully planned.
8. One of the most difficult aspects of the assuming of responsibility has to do with co-operative planning of the agenda.

WE TESTED SOME BELIEFS ABOUT THE BIOGRAPHICAL METHOD[*]

TRESSA BANKS, EDGAR S. FARLEY, OSCAR POWERS, FLOYD VANDERMEER, ROBERT WALDORF, AND STEPHEN M. COREY

Purpose of the Study

This article is a report on some aspects of a co-operative research study conducted by a group of us who teach in the department of social studies of the Battle Creek High School, in collaboration with a consultant from the Horace Mann-Lincoln Institute of School Experimentation of Teachers College, Columbia University. The research represents our attempt to test a belief which we thought should have more influence on the organization and content of our courses in American history. The belief was: If boys and girls can be taught to develop a reasoning admiration for outstanding American historical personages, they will, to a measurable degree, incorporate into their own behavior patterns some of the outstandingly desirable characteristics of these same historic personages. As a consequence of this belief, we decided to put more emphasis on the biographical approach

[*] This report first appeared in *The School Review*, 59:157-163, March 1951. It is reprinted by permission of the authors and *The School Review*.

in the teaching of American history. We agreed, too, that, during the spring semester of 1950, this belief might well be investigated so that we could have some evidence to support our plans for future teaching.

The Hypothesis to Be Tested

During our first two group meetings we worked out a design for an elaborate, complicated, and rather perfectionistic study. It soon became clear that we had planned an investigation which was more than we could handle. This, we believe, will often happen when a group of teachers first undertakes research. Not only were we unaccustomed to investigating our practices, but we had little free time to do so. We had full teaching programs, and, while substitute teachers were provided during our group meetings with the consultant, we soon realized that we would not have time to construct the instruments necessary for a comprehensive inquiry. We also felt inadequate to measure change because of the statistical problems involved. The longer we talked about this matter, the more clearly we realized that studies of change through time were fraught with many difficulties. This was true despite the fact that teaching is undertaken to effect change.

Because we are inexperienced investigators who wanted to test, within the limits of our research ability, the relation between admiration of famous Americans and certain other factors, we finally decided to attempt to test the following hypotheses:

1. A substantial positive correlation will exist between scores measuring information pupils have learned about famous Americans and the extent to which these same persons are admired.

This prediction is based on our belief that we should give more emphasis to the biographical method. In our teaching we spent considerable time relating and discussing items of personal information bearing on the lives of American historic personages. We used the usual techniques—films, filmstrips, biographical novels, and other such devices. In general, our "biographical" method involved different emphases rather than different materials. We spent much time considering with our students such questions as: "Why was —— a great man?" "What were the specific qualities that made this man stand out above others in his period?" By means of discussions of this kind we hoped to lead the pupils to a recognition that great men have certain traits in common and that these traits have been learned.

We stressed the biographical method because of our belief that, if high school pupils come to know the men and women who have had so much to do with our national traditions, they will admire these personages. We were not trying to bring about blind worship. We assumed that the reputations of famous Americans had been earned because of accomplishments. Hence, we hypothesized that learning about these accomplishments would result in admiration.

2. *The degree of admiration for famous American historical personages will be appreciably increased as a consequence of one semester of instruction in American history.*

Our prediction that the pupils would develop increasing admiration for these famous Americans was our one attempt to measure growth—growth, over a period of one semester, in admiration of the persons active during the period of history studied.

3. *A measurable degree of relationship will exist between the degree to which these historical persons are admired and the reputation that pupils have among their peers for behaving in a manner consistent with the traits explaining the admiration.*

There is little point to the kind of admiration we were

trying to teach unless it leads pupils to acquire some of the characteristics of the persons admired. We realized that one semester of part-time work could not bring about radical change in the behavior of high-school pupils. On the other hand, we were convinced that, unless we could procure some evidence of the success of our teaching in this respect, we would be quite in the dark. We might not be bringing about a change at all, or, even worse, we might be teaching in such a way that our pupils would be adversely affected in so far as their own characters were concerned.

Our Measuring Instruments

In order to get some evidence of the degree to which our pupils admired a list of twenty-eight well-known Americans, we asked [them] to react to the following form:

Directions: Listed below are the names of twenty-eight people. Historians have considered their lives to have had a sufficient effect upon the United States to have recorded their activities. You will notice that there is a space (__) at the left of each name, and another space (__) at the right of each name. If you feel any degree of admiration for the person named, put an × in the space at the left. If you dislike the person, or have no feeling about the person, leave the space blank. Do not do anything with the space at the right of each name until you have checked all names for which you feel admiration. Then you will find the directions for the space at the right at the bottom of the page.

(__) John Marshall	(__)	(__) Nathan Hale	(__)
(__) Benjamin Franklin	(__)	(__) George Washington	(__)
(__) Samuel Adams	(__)	(__) Roger Williams	(__)
(__) Paul Revere	(__)	(__) James Madison	(__)
(__) T. Jefferson	(__)	(__) Thomas Paine	(__)
(__) Abraham Lincoln	(__)	(__) Daniel Boone	(__)
(__) Robert E. Lee	(__)	(__) Meriwether Lewis	(__)
(__) Stonewall Jackson	(__)	(__) John Q. Adams	(__)
(__) U. S. Grant	(__)	(__) George R. Clark	(__)
(__) Harriet B. Stowe	(__)	(__) John Brown	(__)
(__) Daniel Webster	(__)	(__) John Paul Jones	(__)
(__) Sam Houston	(__)	(__) Andrew Johnson	(__)
(__) Sir Francis Drake	(__)	(__) William Penn	(__)
(__) Andrew Jackson	(__)	(__) John Smith	(__)

Directions for Right Column.—In the space at the right of each person you indicated that you admired by placing a check mark in the left-hand column, indicate the extent of your admiration by using the following scale:

>   Admire very much 5
>   Admire, but have some reservations 4
>   Lukewarm in admiration 3
>   Little admiration 2
>   Admire merely because others do 1

Thus, if you have a great admiration for George Washington, place a 5 in the space at the right of his name. If you have some admiration, but still have some reservations about the person, place a 4, etc. Rate each person you checked. Rate them in the way you really feel, because there is no "right" or "wrong" in this test.

Other teachers interested in the same problem might have selected different names. This, however, did not seem to us to matter much for the purposes of our study. Scores from this form enabled us to get an over-all "degree of admiration score" by adding the total number of "degree of admiration entries" (right-hand column) and dividing by the total number of persons checked as admirable. In other words, we paid no attention to the exact persons checked. We were interested only in the "average" admiration these boys and girls expressed for the list of twenty-eight persons. This form was administered at the beginning and the end of the spring semester of 1950.

We used a rather simple sociometric questionnaire to find out the reputation the children had among their peers with respect to the following six character traits: determination, honesty, stick-to-it-iveness, high moral values, leadership, hard work. These six were those mentioned most frequently by the pupils in answer to a request to list the outstanding desirable characteristics of those Americans who had made significant contributions to the history of our country. The sociometric questionnaire asked:

> Of all the people in this class whom you feel that you really know, which ones (not more than three) would you rate highest in each of the following character traits?

These sociometric data were obtained at the beginning and the end of the semester. The general-reputation score we used was a weighted total of the number of votes received by each pupil. First choices were weighted 3, second 2, and third 1. This meant that the score for a particular pupil represented a summary of judgments of his peers in respect to a composite of desirable traits. The highest score would imply that the pupil receiving it was voted by his classmates as manifesting to a great extent most or all of the six traits.

In order to determine the extent to which the pupils knew something about the persons they admired, we constructed a matching test, one section of which is reproduced [below].

RECOGNITION OF HISTORIC PERSONAGES

Directions: In the column at the left will be found a list of 30 names of people who were important in the history of the United States. In the column at the right will be found a numbered list of 35 phrases. Place the number of the correct identifying phrase in the space at the left of each name. Because there are 30 names and 35 identifying phrases, five of the identifications will, of course, not be used.

Example: (0) Christopher Columbus 0. Reached West Indies in 1492

NAMES
___ Benjamin Franklin
___ George Washington
___ John Marshall
___ Nathan Hale
___ Samuel Adams
___ Roger Williams
___ Paul Revere
___ James Madison
___ Thomas Jefferson
___ Thomas Paine

IDENTIFYING PHRASES
1. Inventor of first practical steamboat
2. "Father of the Constitution"
3. Founder of Delaware
4. Author of Declaration of Independence
5. Inventor, scientist, statesman, and publisher
6. "I regret that I have but one life to give for my country"
7. Prerevolutionary agitator for freedom
8. Chief Justice of Supreme Court
9. Founder of Rhode Island
10. "Old North Church"
11. Author of *Common Sense*
12. Military leader, statesman, chairman of the Constitutional Convention

The Results[1]

Our prediction that information about American historical personages and admiration of them would be closely related was not at all substantiated by the kind of evidence we obtained. The product-moment correlation between these variables was +.05 for the total group and —.02, —.04, and +.10 for the three classes involved. While we recognize that the instruments used to get this evidence were fallible, the fact remains that we had not attempted, before this study, to get any evidence at all. On the basis, then, of the best information available to us, and pertinent to our specific pupils and teaching practices, the possession of information about historical characters has little effect on admiration of them.

The scores measuring information about these famous Americans were quite variable, ranging from 2 to 30. The means and standard deviations for the three classes involved were: Class 1—mean, 14.9; standard deviation, 5.9. Class 2—mean, 14.5; standard deviation, 5.9. Class 3—mean, 14.2; standard deviation, 6.5. The differences between these classes did not seem to us to be significant.

The data gathered at the beginning of the semester on the degree of admiration for the twenty-eight historic personages were less variable. The mean and standard deviation for the total group were 3.7 and .6. This implies either a high degree of homogeneity within the total population or a lack of discriminatory power of the instrument.

Our second prediction—that one semester of instruction in American history would measurably increase the extent to which the pupils admired famous Americans—was not supported by our evidence. The mean of the scores at the beginning of the semester was 3.70, with a standard deviation of .62. At the end of the semester, the mean was 3.79,

[1] We are indebted to Mr. Clifford Bebell for help in statistical computation.

with a standard deviation of .58. Conceivably, the scores earned at the end of the semester might represent somewhat greater homogeneity, but certainly we did not bring about any appreciable increase in admiration during one semester of instruction. Again, it might be said that our measuring instrument was far from ideal. This we would admit. Again, however, the fact remains that the best evidence we have—and the only evidence to date derived from our own pupils and from measuring the effects of our methods—makes it clear that we are not bringing about one of the important changes in our pupils that we are trying to bring about.

Our last prediction involved the relation between admiration of historical personages and reputation. We anticipated that pupils who tended to admire these Americans would have superior reputations among their peers in respect to the traits that explained their admiration. Again our evidence did not support our belief. The coefficient of correlation between these two variables was $+.07$ for the scores obtained at the beginning of the semester and $+.10$ for those obtained at the end. At neither time would it have been possible to predict a pupil's rank in the group on "admiration" from his rank in the group in "reputation." Those pupils who had the best reputations among their peers might not feel much admiration for the historic personages. Apparently, little of the character of the person admired is incorporated into the behavior of the admirer if our measures have any validity.

The sociometric data indicated substantial stability of reputation throughout a one-semester interval. The correlation between the "pre-" and "post-" reputation scores for the total population was $+.88$, and the means were 11.5 and 12.3, respectively. The acquaintanceship developed over a period of one semester resulted in a slightly larger total of character votes for each pupil. This did not seem to us to be significant. We were interested in the fact, however, that one semester of acquaintance in class led to so little change. We wonder about the opportunities we provided these pupils for becoming acquainted to a degree that would make character judgments meaningful.

Intelligence and the Other Variables

Group intelligence-test scores were available for all the pupils. Because we were interested, incidentally, in determining the relationship between intelligence and (1) information about famous Americans, (2) admiration of these historic personages, and (3) character reputation, we computed correlation coefficients between these variables. The mean intelligence quotient for the total group was 98.3, with a standard deviation of 13. This is somewhat lower than is normally obtained for a group of high-school Juniors.

There was no relationship to speak of between intelligence and the disposition to admire famous Americans. The correlation between these variables was $+.06$ for data at the beginning of the semester and $+.13$ at the end. The relationship between intelligence and character reputation, however, was substantial. The correlations for pre- and post-testing were $+.42$ and $+.46$, respectively. This relationship was about the same as that existing between intelligence and the amount of information the pupils possessed about the historical personages. The latter correlation was $+.45$.

Conclusions

This was our first experience, as a group of social-studies teachers, in getting evidence to test beliefs which had given direction to our teaching. We found the task difficult. In addition to learning that the best evidence we could collect failed to support our convictions, we learned a number of other things. (1) At the beginning of the study, we were all disposed to defend our practices on the basis of personal experiences. Because our experiences had been different, our inferences were different. It was difficult to communicate with persons of different convictions. We did not change one another. (2) This attempt on our part to gather evidence was salutary. As we worked more or less co-operatively on instruments to provide the data we needed, our conceptions regarding what we were trying to do became clearer. We were having a common experience that enhanced communication. (3) As we administered our tests, tabulated our data, and tried to draw generalizations from them, we were impressed by the difficulties faced when conducting research. Most of us had taken education courses purporting to teach research design and statistics. Our conclusion is that, as learning experiences, such courses cannot compare with trying to conduct research on a problem of personal concern.

We are well aware that our procedures and instruments were far from perfect. We will do better next time. What we learned about our own teaching may not be true elsewhere. Nor may what is discovered elsewhere by other teachers be true in Battle Creek. We are convinced that the disposition to study, as objectively as possible, the consequences of our own teaching is more likely to change and improve our practices than is reading about what someone else has discovered regarding the consequences of his teaching. The latter may be helpful. The former is almost certain to be.

CHAPTER IV

Common Sense and Action Research*

It has been said a number of times that those who constantly face practical educational problems have not been disposed to use research in coping with these problems. Teachers, supervisors, and administrators tend to think of educational research as the business of experts. They consider themselves qualified to consume research, but not to engage in it. This conviction is the result of several influences, and it is probably based in part upon a belief that the method of science and the method of common sense are quite different. Practical school people are expected to use common sense in making decisions and evaluating the consequences of their actions, but they are not expected to be scientific.

The sharp distinction, almost a qualitative one, between the method of common sense and the method of science is unrealistic.[1] This chapter examines the relationship between the way practical decisions are usually made and tested and the more rigorous methodology of scientific research. The ex-

* The ideas developed in this chapter appeared in briefer form in an article entitled "Educational Research and the Solution of Practical Problems," *Educational Leadership*, 9:478-484, May 1952.

pression *scientific research* is commonly reserved to describe only those attempts at problem solving or hypothesis testing that result in findings in which great confidence can be placed. But there really is only a relative difference between research and the method commonly employed to solve day-to-day instructional or administrative problems. The casual and subjective method of making practical decisions and appraising their consequences differs from research in the *degree* of care exercised and in the *degree* of confidence that can be placed in results. It is possible to progress, by stages, from the method of problem solving that results in actions in which relatively little confidence can be placed to a method resulting in actions in which a greater degree of confidence can be placed. It is assumed, of course, that everyone wants greater confidence in the consequences of his decisions.

Problem Solving: The Method of Common Sense

The relative difference between the method of common sense and the method of research may be clarified by the following illustration. It assumes a group of high school teachers attempting to solve problems similar to those faced by the group whose experiment in the teaching of history was reported in Chapter III. The conversation at the first departmental meeting of the year held by this group of social studies teachers might run as follows:

_____: I think we ought to do something about the fact that pupils in this school just aren't dependable. At least four members of my last year's American history class cheated on the final examination. I know they did.

_____: You're right. Many of them don't have their assignments in on time, either. When the papers do come in, they're sloppy. The kids are irresponsible. A lot of them lie when they give reasons for absence or handing papers in late.

The conversation continues in this vein for some time. Three or four members of the department are responsible for most of the talk. They are noticeably upset. Their comments sometimes reveal more about them than about their pupils. Two of the teachers appear, at times, to be amused. There seems to be general agreement, however, that the boys and girls are lacking in dependability and have not developed certain other character traits that several members of the department consider important.

The conversation resumes:

____: If we gave more emphasis in our history teaching to the biographies of great Americans—men and women who are honest and dependable and trustworthy—the boys and girls might see how important these traits are.

____: I think so, too. Take Lincoln, for example. If we could show how dependable Lincoln was, and the price he paid to be honest—like the time he walked a long distance to correct a mistake he had made in the store—these kids might learn some good lessons.

____: We ought to emphasize other biographies, too. Washington's, for example. He was known for telling the truth. If we were to stress the biographies of great Americans and the children were to realize how important good character is, I'm sure they'd act differently.

These comments imply that several of the teachers believe that an emphasis on the biographies of famous Americans will improve the character of pupils. It can hardly be said at this stage that a hypothesis is being considered. The values of the biographical method have not been contested.

The conversation continues:

____: I think we're in agreement about the emphasis on biography. Let's see whether we can find some biographical novels and motion pictures that highlight the dependability and honesty of great Americans.

____: I think I'll try that. And whenever I get a chance, I'll talk about episodes in the lives of some of our great Americans to try to make the importance of dependability and honesty more vivid.

———: We must be sure to take some time next spring to find out whether or not this emphasis on biography has had any results.

The final remark indicates that at least one member of the department considers the values claimed for emphasis on the biographical method to be hypothetical. He suggests that the consequences of this emphasis be examined in the spring. No one comments on this suggestion.

Let's assume that the biographies of famous historic personages are stressed by these teachers in various degrees throughout a school year and that eight months later there is a final departmental meeting. Many things have already been discussed, such as the quality of the examinations used and the distribution of grades, and then someone says:

———: We've talked several times this year about our emphasis on biographies in American history classes. Does anyone know whether or not this has had any effect?

———: I'm not sure, but a lot of the boys and girls did seem to be more interested when we talked about biography.

———: I don't know whether it has made any difference or not. My pupils seemed interested, too, but I didn't notice any difference in their dependability when it came to handing in papers or preparing for examinations.

The conversation continues for a while. There seems to be general agreement that the method has worked fairly well. The chairman sums things up:

———: Well, let's try this method again. I think there's everything to gain and nothing to lose. Maybe we can persuade the librarian to buy more good historical novels. We might try, too, to make a little more use of motion pictures.

These discussions, decisions, and actions illustrate the way a great many people handle instructional problems.

Feelings are expressed about certain difficulties, suggestions for overcoming them are made, loosely defined actions are taken, and only casual attention is paid to the results of these actions. The teachers did, however, give at least passing attention to most of the matters that professional educational researchers believe to be important. Their consideration of these "aspects of inquiry," however, was subjective, based on impressions rather than objective evidence.

Defining the Problem

No specific problem was ever identified by the group. The members of the department talked about a large problem area. They were worried because the boys and girls did not meet certain standards of dependability, conscientiousness, honesty, and general moral behavior. No real attempt was made to delimit this broad problem area. Terms like *dependability* and *honesty* were not defined, although they are notoriously ambiguous. Many opinions were expressed about cheating and similar behavior, but no one suggested finding out how much cheating took place and under what circumstances. No one seemed to be interested in establishing a "bench mark" that would make it possible to determine whether or not improvement in character resulted from emphasis on the biographical method.

Hypothesizing

The term *hypothesis* as used in action research refers to a prediction that certain desirable consequences will follow if a particular action is taken. In the illustrative example the action taken was the placing of greater emphasis on the biographical method.

The predicted consequence of placing greater emphasis on the biographical method was general improvement in the character—the dependability and honesty—of the boys and girls. No hypothesis was actually phrased, and the one implied was vague and general. Only as an afterthought did one member of the group suggest that it might be well to find out what the consequences of an emphasis on the biographical method had been. No consideration was given to alternative actions that might represent even better ways of improving character. No one seemed to be familiar with attempts that had been made elsewhere to teach social studies in such a way that the values and behavior of boys and girls would be changed.

In Chapter II attention was called to the fact that suggestions for improving an undesirable situation are usually specific applications of a more comprehensive belief or theory. In this case the suggestion that was made involved giving greater emphasis to the biographical method. The implied belief is that pupils who learn about famous Americans will tend to emulate them. This belief is undoubtedly a special case of a more comprehensive theory about the relation between knowledge and behavior. The relation of the specific action proposal to the more complex system of beliefs and values on which it is based was not discussed at all.

Designing the Test

The members of the group agreed to place greater emphasis on biographies in their teaching. This, in a sense, was the group's conception of an "experimental design" to test its hypothesis. It was a casual, offhand design. There was little discussion of what the various teachers meant by "emphasis on the biographical method." There was no attempt to control this emphasis by deciding in advance how much of it would consist of reading or lecturing or looking at motion pictures. There was no agreement on the biographies that were to be stressed. Each teacher was on his own. At the end of the year no one really knew what changes in teaching had been introduced.

Obtaining Evidence

No one suggested that it would be well to determine the extent to which the boys and girls actually were dishonest or otherwise lacking in dependability. At the autumn meeting, when the decision was made to emphasize the biographical method, one teacher said: "We must be sure to take some time next spring to find out whether or not this emphasis on biography has had any results." There was no discussion of how the group might ascertain the results. There was, in general, not much awareness of the need for objective evidence to determine whether or not the actions taken led to the consequences anticipated. No one called attention to any methods that might be employed to find out whether or not honesty or dependability or character in general had been changed. Reliance was placed entirely on casual recollection and subjective opinion.

Generalizing

At the spring meeting a few minutes were devoted to taking a backward look at what had been done and what the consequences seemed to be. Some teachers had one opinion, and some another. Apparently there was agreement that the plan had worked rather well. This generalization led to the decision that the emphasis on biographies should be tried again during the following year.

The "methodology" these social studies teachers used in attacking a problem that concerned them was not unusual. They did what most practical school people who are dealing with a concrete situation do. In many school systems it would, of course, be easy to cite problem solving of a more scientific sort. For example, the location of new school buildings may involve careful hypothesizing regarding population growth, and the accumulation and careful interpretation of considerable evidence. In solving day-to-day difficulties, however, such investigations are rare. A lack of rigorous methodology in attacking practical problems is not, of course, peculiar to educational practitioners.

Problem Solving: The Method of Action Research

The Battle Creek social studies teachers who tested some of their beliefs about the biographical method (see Chapter III) were more sophisticated in their methodology. An analysis of their attack on the problem follows.

Defining the Problem

The Battle Creek teachers were concerned about the character of their pupils. There was quite a bit of talk about honesty, dependability, and other character traits. Several members of the group, however, realized that they were talking about a problem area, not about a specific problem. After a great deal of discussion, they agreed to use, as a criterion of character, peer judgments within the various classes. The traits concentrated on were determination, honesty, "stick-to-it-iveness," high moral values, leadership, and hard work. These were mentioned most frequently by pupils when they listed the outstanding characteristics of Americans who had made significant contributions to the history of their country. The sociometric judgments, which were obtained at the beginning and end of the school year, gave a measure of pupil status before and after the experiment and made possible a more precise estimate of the effect of the biographical method on character.

This "definition" still left the problem a broad one. The teachers realized that peer judgments were not the only criterion of character. What boys and girls think of one another is important, but the judgments of adults have validity, too, as do self-judgments. It was realized also that the six traits used as a basis for the peer judgments did not include all aspects of character. Recognition of these limitations in problem definition seemed not to create undue anxiety, however. At least these teachers were defining an important problem more carefully than they ever had before. Their attempts to get some facts about a problem and to define it somewhat more precisely are in sharp contrast with what was done by the first group of social studies teachers. Several steps were taken in the direction of the kind of methodology that we have come to call educational research.

Hypothesizing

The Battle Creek teachers also were more rigorous in their hypothesizing. They hypothesized consciously and explicitly. Almost from the beginning their attitude toward the proposed change in their method of teaching American history was that it had promise, certainly, but that its consequences were not assured. The reader will recall that they predicted the following:

1. A substantial positive correlation will exist between scores measuring information pupils have learned about famous Americans and the extent to which these same persons are admired.
2. The degree of admiration for famous American historical personages will be appreciably increased as a consequence of one semester of instruction in American history.
3. A measurable degree of relationship will exist between the degree to which these historical persons are admired and the reputation that pupils have among their peers for behaving in a manner consistent with the traits explaining the admiration.

These hypotheses leave much to be desired if scrutinized from the point of view of the professional educational researcher. "A measurable degree of relationship" is not an illustration of pin-point prediction. The teachers did realize, however, that an experiment involved predictions. They did not have much interest in finding out what others had done in connection with the same problem. Their references to the literature of research and speculation about character education were quite casual. They made no conscious attempt to relate their action hypotheses to any theory of learning or character development. In their attack on the problem, however, especially in the formulation of hypotheses, they did much better than the other group of teachers. And this doing better is very important.

Designing the Test

The Battle Creek teachers talked for a long time about the best way to test their belief that emphasis on the biography of famous Americans would have a beneficial effect on the character of their pupils. The design agreed upon involved trying to find out, at the beginning of the year, (1) how much boys and girls knew about famous Americans, (2) the extent to which these Americans were admired, and (3) the reputation of the youngsters among their peers. "Greater emphasis on the biographical method" was then defined as involving the introduction, in all American history classes, of certain readings dealing with the character of famous Americans. A limited number of motion pictures, which all boys and girls would see, was also selected. Each member of the staff agreed to relate to his class, whenever an occasion presented itself, incidents from the lives of famous Americans that called attention to their character. The plan also involved repeating the sociometric tests at the end of the year and comparing "before" and "after" scores. This, the teachers thought, would enable them to find out how much the boys and girls had learned, the extent to which their admiration for famous Americans had changed, and the extent to which their reputation among their peers for the traits agreed upon had been affected.

This design was far from perfect. There was no real agreement among the teachers regarding the time that would be devoted to emphasizing biography or the teaching methods that would be employed. No attempts were made to see what might happen to a control group receiving a year of the usual instruction in American history. But in spite of these obvious limitations, the design represents real progress from subjective, casual, nonscientific inquiry toward careful, thoughtful research procedures.

Obtaining Evidence

One indication of the superiority of the problem solving methods employed by the Battle Creek social studies teachers was their attempt to get evidence—to get facts. They obtained some rather reliable data describing the status of the boys and girls in respect to a number of factors at the beginning and at the end of the school year. Less dependence was placed on casual recall. The instruments used to obtain evidence were of limited reliability, but attempts were made to find out how dependable they were. Little was done to determine the validity of the measuring instruments—the extent to which they really measured what the teachers wanted to measure. Despite these limitations, the realization that facts are essential to the definition of a problem and the testing of action hypotheses, and the willingness to try to obtain these facts, represent a good long step in the direction of better research procedures.

Generalizing

The results were examined at a departmental meeting at the end of the year, and the teachers got help from a consultant who had had experience in interpreting statistical data. They concluded that (1) the possession by pupils of information about historic personages had little effect on their admiration of these personages; (2) one semester of instruction in American history, with emphasis on biographies, did not measurably increase the extent to which boys and girls admired famous Americans; (3) there was no relationship between the extent to which boys and girls admired famous Americans and the reputation they had among their peers for the traits that explained their admiration.

These conclusions were rather disturbing. Admittedly, they were based on measuring instruments and a design that were fallible. There was a strong tendency, too, to overgeneralize and lose sight of the specific circumstances of the inquiry, which should establish the limits for inference. But the conclusions were inferred from better evidence and a better method of problem solving than the group had used before. Consequently, considerable confidence was placed in them.

In the above review of the action research conducted by the Battle Creek teachers several limitations have been pointed out. Some readers, especially those who know a great deal about the design of traditional educational research, have undoubtedly identified additional weaknesses and have said to themselves, Why didn't someone tell them? Why spend all this time doing research if it can't be good research? Conclusions based on fallible procedures are bad conclusions.

These questions and the final comment are important. They are frequently voiced when individuals or groups report the action research they have engaged in to improve their decisions and to evaluate the practices resulting from these decisions. The answer to the question, Why didn't someone tell them? is that someone did. Whether or not these research suggestions were accepted and understood and acted upon, however, depended on a number of factors. Most important of these was the basic motivation for undertaking the inquiry at all, namely, the desire to teach American history in such a way that the character of the pupils would be improved. If suggestions about design and statistical treatment of data seemed to the teachers to lead them away from their main interest, the suggestions were overlooked. Another factor was the time available. Practical judgments were constantly being made about the desirability of research refinements that required a great deal of additional time. All the members of the group had full teaching schedules. Finally, no suggestion about research procedures got more than courteous attention unless it made sense to the researchers. In other words, if their general experience, re-examined and re-evaluated, did not support the arguments advanced to defend the research refinements, nothing happened. No grades were involved. Extrinsic motivational devices were not available.

The contention that educational research should not be undertaken unless it can be good research is a vague one. Advocating that a group engage in the best research it is capable of and strive for improvement in the future has much greater meaning. The research capabilities of the members of a group are conditioned by their previous experience with scientific problem solving, the time they have available to study their teaching, the other important jobs they have to do, and the ways they have reached decisions and evaluated actions in the past.

The argument that conclusions based on fallible research methods are fallible conclusions is true. The important point, however, is that better research results in better conclusions.

Conclusion

An attempt has been made in this chapter to indicate that the quality of inquiry resulting in decisions and actions is relative. No research conforms to absolute standards of quality. Excellent research involves a method of inquiry that warrants a high degree of confidence in its results. All problem solving, however, involves defining the problem, hypothesizing, developing a design to test the hypotheses, getting evidence, and generalizing from this evidence. If the quality of the definition, hypothesis, design, evidence, and generalization is high, the over-all action research is good—that is, it will lead to actions in which the investigators may place confidence. Some investigations illustrate advanced techniques in certain of these aspects of inquiry and careless techniques in others. Much of the research of professional educational investigators, for example, illustrates naive generalizing. This is most apparent in connection with the kinds of assumptions about sampling that are made in order to use conventional statistical formulas. Sampling practices frequently are in sharp conflict with these assumptions.

One limitation of most of the writing and talking about educational inquiry is the implication that it is not research unless it closely approximates several methodological absolutes. The fact that attempts at problem solving fall at various points on a continuum ranging from careless, untested inquiry to careful and reliable research is rarely emphasized. This is regrettable because, although teachers and other school people value research in the abstract, they feel that it has little relation to the methods they must employ to solve their own problems. There is little motivation for practical people who are trying to solve practical problems to move in the direction of better and better research methods. No one has a corner on these better methods. They are learned with practice. To refrain from trying because one lacks skill or has perfectionist aspirations precludes improvement, and improvement is what counts.

NOTES TO

CHAPTER IV

1. An interesting chapter on the similarities and differences between common sense and scientific inquiry is included in Dewey's *Logic: The Theory of Inquiry* (33, p. 60-80). Dewey considers the problem historically and goes more deeply into it than most authors. He concludes by contending that "the basic problem of present culture and associated living is that of effecting integration where division now exists." (33, p. 79) He is referring here to the importance of recognizing "the fundamental unity of the structure of inquiry in common sense and science . . . ." (33, p. 79)

CHAPTER V

Conditions Favorable to Action Research*

Most of the Horace Mann-Lincoln Institute staff members work in field situations with public school personnel on cooperative action research projects. We have done this for the past eight years, and we now know more than we did about some of the general conditions that encourage action-oriented curricular experimentation. This chapter describes some of the conditions and suggests what might be done to create them. The suggestions are addressed chiefly to supervisors and administrators, because an atmosphere that supports curricular experimentation is much more likely to be developed if status leaders favor it.

It probably is not necessary to call attention again to the fact that using the best methods of scientific inquiry to solve practical problems is not easy. Recommending that other people do so does not necessarily imply much conviction. In the Institute we have tried hard to practice what we advocate, namely, an action research approach to the solution of practical problems. When we are our better

---

* Some of the material in this chapter first appeared in *Educational Administration and Supervision*, 36:209-216, April 1950, under the title "Conditions Conducive to Curricular Experimentation."

selves, we are continuously testing, in action situations, the worth of hypotheses that have to do with our own ways of working.[1]

Freedom to Admit Limitations

There is little likelihood that curricular experimentation will occur in school systems unless teachers, administrators, and supervisors have an appreciable degree of freedom and willingness to admit and talk about the jobs that trouble them. In some schools and in some school systems there is little tendency to speak frankly about those parts of the program that are not going well. Persons who are intimately associated with relatively unsuccessful practices are even less likely to talk about the limitations of these practices.

The reasons for this reluctance to discuss failures are numerous. Most people have learned that when they are in difficulties, it is safer to admit nothing, or at most very little. It is easier to become skillful at projecting responsibility for failure onto others, or onto external circumstances. This is not necessarily done, of course, with any conscious intent to find a scapegoat. Admitting mistakes—especially admitting them publicly—involves risks to one's ego, and sometimes to one's economic security, that are just too great to face.

The actions of the status leaders in a school system—the superintendent, principal, supervisor—are of crucial importance in this connection.[2] When these persons are able to discuss their problems and inadequacies, teachers find it easier to do so. The successful administrator, however, is supposed to be one who knows what he wants done and gets someone else to do it with dispatch. This stereotype is almost always a part of the self-picture of those with leadership responsibilities in education, and it enables few administrators to feel they can safely talk about areas of their work in which they feel inadequate.[3] The reports published by many school superintendents, describing the state of public education in their own school system, are consistent with this stereotype. These reports generally call attention to the victories, gloss over the failures, and by indirection imply that the administrator's talents are of a high order. The reader is given the impression that the situation is well in hand.

In their relations with teachers, many status leaders imply, first, that they themselves have few serious limitations, and, second, that they stand ready and willing to help teachers with their many difficulties. This attitude almost forces teachers to assume the same attitude, although they rarely add that they are ready and willing to help administrators. In-service education, as a number of people have remarked, is ordinarily a one-way street.

In schools where teachers are reluctant to discuss their professional problems with one another, and where the administrators rarely admit to teachers that they, too, are having difficulties, a sort of impasse exists. Someone has to take the initiative to break the circle. This initiative might well be taken by the status leaders, who constitute a smaller group and presumably have greater security. Certainly they have larger salaries and are supposed to "set an example."

Some time ago twelve high school teachers and their principal were discussing the tenth-grade core program and its improvement. Almost no progress was made because the teachers were unable to talk freely about problems involved in the program. No one seemed to be able to take the initiative in expressing dissatisfaction with his own teaching. To do so would have been equivalent to a public confession of failure, and no one finds it easy to confess limitations unless it is probable that the others in the group will also confess theirs.

This situation changed rather dramatically when the principal called attention to some problems that he was facing in connection with the program. He made it clear that he was baffled, admitted that he did not feel secure in working with the group, and said that he would appreciate whatever help the twelve teachers could give him.

Only a few minutes after this statement by the status leader, a number of teachers—not all of them—began to express themselves more freely about the kind of help they hoped they might get from the principal. They obviously were not hostile. His candor and evident sincerity evoked support, not attack. From this the conversation soon shifted to other difficulties the teachers were having, which they alone could do something about.

Some risks are taken, certainly, by the status leader who talks about his limitations, even if he makes it clear that he wants to do better. His admissions may be used against him by people who achieve some security and self-importance by criticizing their leaders. Teachers who are anxious because of their own limitations may be quite ready to report that "the principal himself admits he doesn't know what this is all about." This risk must be taken, however, because the alternative may be curricular stagnation.[4]

If a status leader who has not been in the habit of confiding his professional problems to teachers suddenly does so at a staff meeting, he may be listened to rather skeptically by a number of the people present. They will want to test his sincerity, or at least see it tested, before they commit themselves. They will want to be shown, for example, that the principal's request for help results in genuine and positive consideration of the suggestions made. In other words, the admission of limitations by a status leader is not likely to be successful as a technique or trick for getting others to admit theirs—not for very long, anyway.

It is not only the status leader, of course, who can take the initiative in admitting difficulties. Anyone who feels safe enough to be somewhat honest and reasonably humble and objective in talking about his own instructional or curricular problems can start things going. Most of us give sufficient critical attention to the limitations of others. It is unlikely that this criticism will persuade them to engage in much action research to improve their decisions and practices. It may, however, persuade them to engage in some creative and informal experimentation designed to put the critic in his place.

Much has been written and said in recent years about the importance of a permissive atmosphere in cooperative curriculum development.[5] At times the impression is given that this kind of psychological climate is good for its own sake. Maybe it is, but few things are. The permissive atmosphere is valuable primarily because it enables people to come closer to expressing the truth, as they see it, in what they say, without running the unbearable risk of being struck down. An increasingly scientific approach to the solution of important instructional problems depends on the ability of school people to speak freely what is on their mind. A permissive group climate makes it easier to get some of the hidden agenda items out into the open, where they can be looked at and dealt with. As Bradford has stated, all groups work on two levels. On one level is the acknowledged and formally designated group task. It is the public agenda. But there is a second level:

> Unlabelled, private and covered, but deeply felt and very much the concern of the group, is another level. Here are all of the conflicting motives, desires, aspirations and emotional reactions held by the group members (including the leader), sub-groups, or the group as a whole that cannot be fitted legitimately into the accepted group task. Here are all the problems which, for a variety of reasons, cannot be laid on top of the table. (7, p. 3)

Opportunities to Invent

Widespread experimentation or action research will not suddenly appear just because people are speaking frankly about the problems they are facing in connection with their work. A second characteristic of school systems in which curricular experimentation is being carried on is the provision of many opportunities for developing creative ideas about new and promising practices or materials. This is the hypothesizing aspect of action research.

One way of encouraging creative invention is to make it possible for people to develop and test their ideas against the experience of other people. Institutionalized public education tends to be conservative, and sessions in which people let themselves go and forget the past for the time being often result in genuinely creative ideas.

It is difficult to overestimate the importance, for curricular experimentation, of numerous opportunities for creative and free discussion. These discussions bring new and promising ideas into the open and develop an *esprit de corps* which makes the innovator feel less lonely. Consideration of change is often threatening because it implies an admission of difficulty. When an actual experiment, in the broadest sense, is suggested, another threat is introduced. Any contemplated change makes explicit the need for learning new values and new practices. Such learnings are often difficult.

Discussions of professional problems are more likely to be creative and adventuresome if the participants know one another personally as well as professionally. Fear of unfriendly criticism is a powerful inhibitor. Everyone has probably been surprised and impressed by the creativity of associates seen for the first time under circumstances that encouraged them to be free and made them feel liked and accepted.

Differences of opinion between individuals who are professional acquaintances only are threatening because each person is often criticizing the only thing he knows about the other. When differences of opinion about educational theory or practice, or anything else, are expressed by persons who have had an opportunity to become acquainted personally and to like one another, the controversy does not threaten to sever the only bond holding these people together. Similarly, the consequences are not damaging if a "crazy" idea is advanced seriously among friends. They may even keep the idea from being tried out.

This is one reason why many status leaders and teachers who want not only experimentation but good human relations in general have taken steps to create a friendly, permissive atmosphere for professional meetings. Even something as seemingly superficial as serving tea or coffee may help. The recent emphasis on improvement of the group process represents, in part, a more fundamental attempt to make an exchange of experiences fruitful.[6] If group work is to be maximally effective, people must know, trust, respect, and understand one another.[7]

Rogers has made an interesting suggestion in relation to hearing, and reacting to, criticisms of ideas in group discussion situations. He contends that a major barrier to communication is the persistent tendency to evaluate ideas without understanding them, and he urges an experiment:

> The next time you get into an argument with your wife, or your friend, or with a small group of friends, just stop the discussion for a moment and for an experiment institute this rule: "Each person can speak up for himself only *after* he has first restated the ideas and feelings of the previous speaker accurately, and to that speaker's satisfaction." (70, p. 4)

Several Institute staff members have tested this idea with groups of school people, and it seems to have great promise. Something like Rogers' experiment was tried in one group with rather dramatic consequences. An argument had developed between an elementary school teacher, who insisted that she and her colleagues did a good job of teaching boys and girls to read, and a secondary school teacher, who complained because he thought the children came from the elementary schools without having learned how to read. Finally the chairman said to the elementary school teacher: "Mary, I'd like to hear you summarize, if you will, your understanding of Paul's position as a secondary school teacher." This stopped Mary. She hadn't really been listening to Paul. She had realized only that he was attacking her, and she was fighting back. She made an effort to express his point of view, however, and asked the secondary school teacher whether what she had said represented what he had had in mind. He corrected her a bit but finally admitted that she had described his position adequately.

The chairman then turned to the secondary school teacher and asked him to summarize the position of the elementary school teacher. After he had done so, there did not seem to be a great deal to argue about. Each of these two people, after trying conscientiously to see the problem as his opponent did, found that he had developed some appreciation of the other's point of view. Although this technique will not, of course, eliminate all arguments, it will tend to clarify issues and reduce conflict resulting from misunderstanding.

Discussions and group meetings are not the only activities that encourage the development of creative ideas. Reading professional literature (including reports of traditional research studies), visiting the classes of other teachers, attending professional meetings, studying motion pictures, all may help teachers and administrators think of different and possibly better ways of doing things—help them hypothesize. Unless these different ideas about practices and teaching materials can be developed as pictures in somebody's mind, there can be no action hypotheses to test.

Encouragement to "Try It Out"

The identification of professional problems and the search for better ways of getting jobs done contribute little to curriculum change unless teachers who have developed promising innovations are encouraged to try them out. Freedom to try out new ideas is a third characteristic of schools in which the curriculum is being improved through experimentation. To provide encouragement, resources, and materials for teachers who want to initiate and test new and promising practices is one way for status leaders to make it clear that they value thoughtful experimentation. When teachers are supported up to the point of actually changing the curriculum, and then the support is withdrawn, their reaction is very likely to be, "What's the use? We meet and talk and plan, and nothing happens."

The status leader plays a crucial role in providing encouragement for the experimenting teacher. Whatever he can do to support and understand those who are willing to test their ideas in practice will have beneficial consequences. It is assumed, of course, that the new idea is promising; that it has been tested against the ideas of other creative teachers and leaders, who agree it is worth trying out in a real situation; and that the relationship among the teachers and leaders is such that the person suggesting the innovation will be able to hear, and react to, criticisms of it.

Building the morale of teachers who want to experiment may not be, in practice, an unmixed blessing. It may result in lowering the morale of teachers who do not consider what they are doing "experimental." This hazard is reduced if the status leader, and others, have a broad conception of experimentation or action research. In Chapter IV the idea was developed that action research represents little more than a refinement of a process every teacher goes through as he tries to improve. The stereotype of teachers as people who can have the same year of experience for any number of consecutive years applies to a very small minority. Almost everyone occasionally tries out some new ideas that seem to him, at least, to have greater promise. And some sort of evidence is sought on which an estimate of the worth of these new practices, and the desirability of continuing or modifying them, can be based. This is the essence of action research. It is not that some teachers experiment and others do not. Some teachers experiment more consciously and more carefully than others, and it is this careful and conscious experimentation that the administrator will want to encourage.

Improvement in Methods of Group Work

At times, teachers who like to try out new ideas may be seen as threats by those of their peers who think of experimentation as something that may force them to change against their will. Pupils, too, are frequently resistant to changes in what they have come to believe is appropriate classroom procedure. Many teachers who have tried to involve their pupils in classroom planning have met this kind of resistance.

The deterring influence of some of these factors can be reduced if groups of teachers experiment cooperatively. In numbers there is strength, and greater talent. This point was developed in Chapter II, but nothing was said about what might be done to improve the processes of group work. The members of the Horace Mann-Lincoln Institute staff are constantly meeting problems because we, and the people in the field who are cooperating with us, have not yet learned enough about ways and means of facilitating *cooperative* experimentation. Most of us can talk with considerable persuasiveness about what ought to be done, but there is a great difference between having mastered the vocabulary of group work and practicing the behavior this vocabulary implies. Experience is almost certain to modify talk, but talk frequently has little effect on subsequent practice.

Reports of a number of projects in which groups tried to improve the curriculum cooperatively indicate that four conditions must exist, at least in some degree, before the quality of cooperation can improve.[8] These conditions are:

1. Freedom to change the established ways of working in groups.
2. Continuous evaluation of group processes by group members.
3. Willingness to put into effect those changes which various members of the group, after considerable discussion, feel are necessary if the methods of group work are to be improved.
4. Training in group work methods under circumstances that simulate reality but are not quite so crucial.

Freedom to Change Methods of Group Work

Probably everyone has been baffled by the persistence of certain group work methods with which no one seems to be satisfied but about which no one seems to feel free to do anything. There are schools where the habitual method of conducting staff meetings makes little sense either to the principal or to the teachers, but the method is re-employed every time the staff meets. The agenda is set by the principal; he always chairs the meeting; motions are made, seconded, discussed, passed or rejected in a desultory fashion, and often forgotten.[9] No one is happy about the situation, but there apparently is a degree of security in doing what always has been done.

The status leader can play a decisive part in changing this pattern. He is in the best position to create an atmosphere that encourages some freedom to change, since he is usually viewed by the teachers as having established the current practice. An action as simple as arranging for someone else to chair staff meetings may initiate improvements. Another action that encourages freedom is self-criticism and a request for help by the status leader in a group situation. This does not mean that complete candor is advisable at the beginning; perhaps, in this kind of situation, it never is. If everyone reported exactly what he thought about staff or committee meetings *in the meetings,* the consequences might be disastrous. There is not much likelihood that this will ever happen. Most people test the limits rather gingerly when, for the first time, they feel some freedom to express what they really think about meetings or other group work.

Anyone might suggest that the habitual way of conducting staff or committee meetings be examined, but if the person with higher status takes the initiative, more is likely to happen. Teachers are reluctant to express publicly, in the presence of all the people involved, their feelings about group work in their own schools. Everyone knows, of course, that they express themselves rather freely to one another. All too frequently, however, this kind of expression results in little more than the release of hostilities.

Evaluation of Group Processes by Group Members

Trying to find out how a group work session has gone from the people involved in it makes so much sense that it is hard to understand why it is so rarely done. It is a wise investment of time to take five or ten minutes at the end of a meeting in order to raise questions such as the following: "Have we gone about this job in the best way? . . . What might we have done, and what should we do in the future, to make our work more expeditious? . . . How do we feel about our accomplishments during this meeting?" If the atmosphere is such that oral answers to these questions will not be freely given, they can be put in writing and remain anonymous.

A number of groups have experimented with a variety of forms for obtaining these post-meeting evaluations, or post-meeting reactions. In the beginning the forms should be as simple as possible. Many groups with which members of the Institute staff have worked use only these two questions:

1. Please check your over-all feeling about the success of this meeting:

    > 5—Very successful
    > 4—Rather successful
    > 3—So-so
    > 2—Not very successful
    > 1—Just a waste of time

2. Write a sentence or so in which you state your reasons for reacting as you did.

A subcommittee of the total group then tabulates the responses, reports them back to the group as soon as possible, and recommends changes that are inferred from the individual replies. This, admittedly, is just a start; and it will be a false start unless something is done as a result of the evaluations obtained.

Many forms are available for getting individual reactions to group processes. Some of these are long and complicated.[10] It is not only useless but sometimes quite hazardous to introduce an involved post-meeting reaction form to people unaccustomed to giving the type of reaction the form calls for. The degree of penetration of the post-meeting inquiry should be determined by the readiness of the group to render the judgments required and use the evidence that results. There are many advantages in having the kinds of questions asked on the post-meeting reaction form and the use to be made of the responses determined by the group as a whole. During initial evaluation efforts little is gained by reference to expressions such as *group dynamics*. As a matter of fact, exotic terminology may act as a deterrent to self-analysis.

It might be said in passing that getting judgments from the members of a group about the success with which their work has been conducted is one of the most sensible and tangible ways of introducing action research procedures into group work on school problems. The post-meeting reaction data usually suggest some promising changes; these can be put into effect, and their consequences tested by subsequent post-meeting reactions.

Willingness to Try Out Proposed Improvements

That the data from the post-meeting reaction forms are usually rich sources of proposals for improvement has already been pointed out. The comments may range from suggested changes in the membership of working groups to expressions of concern about the feasibility of putting group recommendations into practice. Actually doing something with these suggestions is essential if they are to continue to be made. One of the first things to do is to consider with the entire group the desirability of effecting the changes that have been suggested by a few people. If it has no other value, this kind of discussion serves to make the members of the group more keenly aware of the methods they are using to get their work done.

Training in Group Work Methods

Trying out new methods of group work under realistic circumstances and appraising the consequences is, of course, highly beneficial.[11] Frequently, however, group members are reluctant to try out new procedures because they feel insecure and realize that they lack some of the skills required for giving these procedures a fair trial. There is therefore a great advantage in arranging for training sessions that have as their sole purpose the development of skills that will facilitate group work. A few of the things that happen as a result of such training are described in Chapter VI of this book. The members of the Institute staff have had considerable success in field situations with one-day training conferences for group leaders.[12] A training program that involved only one half-day meeting per month for seven months was judged to be effective by the participants.

Improving methods of group work is analogous in some respects to improving reading. Some techniques are more effective than others. Almost anything, however, that makes the importance of group process apparent and results in giving attention to better working methods brings about improvement.

Concern with Obtaining Evidence

Another characteristic of schools engaged in fruitful curricular experimentation is their concern with evidence. Evidence is essential to experimentation. It is one of the chief differentiating factors between practices more or less casually tried out and action research. The results of many educational experiments and innovations have been controversial because inadequate provision was made for obtaining data describing their success or failure. Those who substitute for the "tried and true" newer and presumably more promising practices are under an especial obligation to obtain objective evidence about consequences.

Curricular experimenters place themselves at the mercy of the evidence, and this demands considerable courage. Sometimes "experiments" are announced with the clear implication that if they do not succeed, someone will get into trouble. Every experiment cannot be successful. If expectations were invariably fulfilled, there would be no need to experiment.

Determining the consequences of curricular experimentation need not be as complicated and difficult as some of the textbooks on measurement and evaluation imply. This idea is developed at greater length in Chapter VII. Some evidence is better than no evidence. Few traditional educational practices are buttressed by research data appropriate to the specific situations in which the practices are being employed. Almost anything the innovator does to obtain objective data describing the success or failure of his experiment moves him in the right direction. Accumulating voluminous data describing the consequences of comprehensive educational modifications is difficult. It is particularly difficult if standards of perfection are constantly held up. When teachers experiment, they are seeking, not complete and final evidence, but evidence better than that previously available. Teachers starting curricular experimentation usually think more carefully about evidence if each claim for the value of a proposed innovation leads to consideration of the kinds of data that can be gathered to test the claim.

Time and Resources for Experimentation

A final condition essential to action research designed to improve the curriculum is the provision of time and other resources. If teachers are expected to study their activities and experiment with promising innovations, current ideas of what they should do during the school day need careful re-examination. When courses of study are prescribed, and teachers are expected to follow directions and teach from textbooks or laboratory manuals or workbooks, they can meet one class after another, day after day, with few interruptions other than those needed to recover energy and relax. The situation is quite different when teachers are expected to study their teaching. They will then need time during the regular school day to think, to plan, to gather and interpret data, to discover or create and bring together the new resources needed for the experimentation, and to do the many other things that are involved in a research approach to the improvement of teaching. When teachers are expected to do all these extras on their own time, while carrying a teaching load originally designed to consume all of their energy, little happens.

When time for research is made available, important things do happen. In one school in which action research has been going on for several years, additional staff members were employed to free each of the members of the research team for one period a day.[13] As a result, a new tenth-grade general education program was developed, which could be defended on the basis of an unusual amount of evidence. In other schools with which members of the Horace Mann-Lincoln Institute are cooperating, substitute teachers take over the classes of their experimenting colleagues at regular intervals to enable the investigating groups to meet.[14] Several similar plans are feasible, and they all require additional funds. The experience of the Institute and the schools associated with it has been that such additional funds are well spent.

The importance of providing material aid for teachers who want to experiment need hardly be stressed. Many innovations require new instructional material, additional mimeographing, furniture and schedule modifications, improved evaluation instruments, or additional funds for clerical assistance. Experimenting teachers, receiving $3,500 a year for their teaching talents, too frequently do clerical work that might well be done by a high school graduate receiving a salary of $1,800.

Reference has been made a number of times to the importance of providing adequate consultant services for teachers who are experimenting. As part of their in-service education program, many schools and school systems now spend appreciable sums of money for consultation. Rarely, however, is provision made for employing persons who are especially qualified as curriculum action research consultants—persons who have had extensive and successful experience in working with teachers who are trying to improve instruction by a method involving careful problem definition, creative hypothesizing, systematic initiation of promising practices, and accumulation of evidence to test their worth.

Because research is a necessary part of this method of solving instructional problems, the consultant who can be most helpful must have unusual talents. Collier writes:

> But let me emphasize that this kind of research makes demands on the research worker that are far more severe than those made by the specialized and isolated kind. It requires of him a more advanced and many-sided training, and in addition a type of mind and personality which can sustain, in suspension, complex wholes, and which can entertain—yes, and be drawn and impelled by—human values and policy purposes while yet holding them disinterestedly far away. (18, p. 300 f.)

One aspect of the consultant's role is emphasized by everyone who has served in this capacity to groups of teachers engaged in experimentation. The action research consultant must be an active collaborator, not only a resource in the ordinary sense. He is personally involved in the action research because of his desire to improve the social situation. He is a member of the research team, which includes himself as a research specialist, the persons whose behavior must change if the problem is to be solved, and persons in administrative positions.

Conclusion

The attention given in this chapter to the six conditions favorable to curricular experimentation implies a belief about the improvement of the curriculum. This belief is that the experiences boys and girls have in a school will be most worth while if many teachers are trying out promising ideas and studying the consequences of putting them into practice. An alternative method of curriculum improvement is the conventional one of course-of-study building by a small central committee dominated by status leaders. Although this method frequently results in impressive bulletins, it often leads to little significant curriculum change.

NOTES TO CHAPTER V

1. Several major studies have been conducted by Institute staff members in cooperation with our research associates in the field to enable us to make sounder decisions and engage in better practices. See Coffman (17), Cunningham (29), Halverson (42), Lawler (50), Lowe (55), Mackenzie, Corey, and associates (57), and Wann (78).

2. In connection with the Horace Mann-Lincoln Institute Leadership Studies, conducted in collaboration with the Denver, Colorado, high school principals and coordinators, Mackenzie, Corey, and associates (57) considered at some length the relationship between status and in-service growth.

3. The school administrator's conception of himself influences his ability to admit limitations and his desire to change. Individual differences are, of course, great. Some of the principals and supervisors studied by Corey and Halverson (27) were, assuming that the inventory used is valid, almost completely satisfied with their interpersonal relations behavior.

4. Someone should write a thoughtful article on "Teachers as Threats to Administrators." The frequency with which administrators inhibit and threaten teachers is often emphasized, but the threat is almost always reciprocal. The inhibiting influence of the person with higher official status is simply more obvious and, overtly, more powerful.

5. For about ten years the importance of free and informal interpersonal staff relations has been emphasized in books on curriculum and supervision. See Caswell and associates (12, chap. v), Gwynn (41, p. 731 f.), Koopman, Miel, and Mis-

ner (48), Krug (49, chap. vii), McNerney (60, chap. i), Miel (61), and Smith, Stanley, and Shores (71, Part IV).

6. The volume by Benne and Muntyan (3) is a rich source of ideas for making cooperative curriculum work more effective.

7. Understanding the other person's point of view requires skill in discerning his perceptions and the ability to put oneself in his place. For a discussion of this problem see Corey, Foshay, and Mackenzie (26).

8. Anyone who wishes to go more deeply into this subject can find many references in Benne and Muntyan (3). The June 1952 issue of *Adult Leadership* (vol. 1, no. 2) includes some interesting ideas as well as selected bibliographies.

9. Knowles (47) describes, in a humorous but penetrating way, many of the limitations of the parliamentary method of getting group work done.

10. Reference has been made several times to *Adult Leadership,* a monthly publication of the Adult Education Association of the United States of America. It is a new magazine, but it promises to be a practical and helpful journal for people interested in group work. The June 1952 issue, "Spotlight on Leadership," suggests a number of excellent ideas and methods. One is a long check list—fifteen items—designed to help a group take a look at its own ways of working.

11. The literature on leadership training through the use of laboratory or role-playing situations is rather extensive. See Corey (25), Liveright (54, chap. ix), and Maier (58, chaps. iv and v).

12. Our experience with a one-day training session for group leaders is described by Corey, Halverson, and Lowe (28). A briefer report is by Doll, Halverson, and Lowe (35).

13. Evans (37) describes in greater detail how arrangements were made in Battle Creek, Michigan, for giving teachers sufficient time for experimentation.

14. Foshay, Wann, and associates (39) refer to the "substitute teacher teams" that did so much to facilitate action research in Springfield, Missouri.

CHAPTER VI

Action Research as a Way to Learn*

This chapter reports some of the collective thinking and research of thirteen students and two instructors in a seminar held during the second semester of the academic year 1950–51. The seminar, part of the program of the Horace Mann-Lincoln Institute of School Experimentation, was designed to provide training for action research consultants.

As members of the seminar group, we were primarily concerned with the human relations problems faced in consultation of this kind. In order to learn more about action research as well as the human relations problems faced by

* The total manuscript of which this chapter is an abstract is seventy-six pages long and includes a number of reports of cooperative seminar activities. The formulation of the hypotheses, the design of the inquiries, and the determination of ways of getting evidence resulted from group activity. Subcommittees were formed to write each report, and the rough drafts were criticized by the entire group. The several reports were then combined into one manuscript by the author and his Institute associate in the seminar, Arthur W. Foshay.

The student members of the seminar were:

William Carlisle	Paul M. Halverson	Paul Riley
William Cotton	Charles Latimer	Lamaimas Saradatta
Lucille Field	Howard Leavitt	Abraham Shumsky
Alexander Frazier	Elizabeth Lowe	Mary Ullman
	Laura Mixner	

a research consultant, we decided to conduct action research to improve our own functioning. Our experience differed considerably from the conventional teaching-learning procedures employed in advanced courses for supervisors. The seminar activities are described here in some detail because they may be suggestive to others who wish to modify their ways of working with students in teacher-training classes. Several members of the group have subsequently used action research successfully in their undergraduate and graduate instruction.

Our procedure usually involved the identification of a problem, the formulation of hypotheses stated as proposed courses of action for dealing with the problem, and the subsequent testing of these hypotheses through analysis of their consequences. We tried hard to generalize continuously. In order to study our actions, we used a variety of methods for getting evidence—inventories, transcriptions, questionnaires, verbatim typescripts, pictures, tape recordings, and thoughtful but subjective reports of learnings. Our analyses of the evidence were both quantitative and qualitative. Because we were primarily interested in improving our own insights and ways of working, we made few attempts to extrapolate our findings to a larger population.

Reading of references constituted a minor part of our learning activity. We believed that we could best learn to improve our own human relations behavior as research consultants by trying out among ourselves promising activities—frequently novel to us—and studying the consequences. As has been said, we constantly searched for generalizations and insights that might be inferred both from the evidence of our action research and from our past experiences.

The way we went about our learning—trying to test our hunches in action, studying the consequences, and generalizing—was an unusual and rewarding experience for us. We all had completed more than two years of graduate study and were familiar with the design of traditional educational research and the effect on our behavior of reading reports of this research. Most of us had never before, however, been members of a group that conducted research in order to improve its own behavior. We had become somewhat disillusioned about the value of learning experiences limited to talking and reading about interpersonal relations.

The sequence of our seminar research activities was not determined in advance. One inquiry grew out of another. For example, our consideration of the human relations problems faced by the research consultant brought us quickly to a study of the influence of status factors. Accordingly, we began our semester's work by studying the meaning of status in a problem-centered working group. After we had reached some agreement on the meaning of terms, we turned to a problem that arises in connection with the status factor— hostility to the status person. Here we attempted to crystallize our learnings by role-playing some of the problem situations and predicting and testing the effect of various kinds of behavior on hostility.

Hostility in a group is a problem in itself. We were interested in the polarizing, or taking of sides, that often results from the expression of hostilities, and our next study centered on a situation involving a group that included two members basically contemptuous of each other. Tension within a group continued to interest us, and so we next studied a single example of such tension—that resulting from domination by a compulsive talker.

Consideration of the roles played in a group, which was a recurring topic of interest, led us to an examination of one role that seemed particularly helpful in resolving conflicts and making groups productive—the role of "summarizer." We then returned to a more direct consideration of the problem of interpersonal tensions. This time we examined the possibility that much tension is the product of hurts, consciously or unconsciously administered to one another by members of a group. Our last activity was to appraise the semester's work. We examined not only its influence on our thinking but also its effect on our behavior.

What we did was to spiral around the general problem of human relations as one element of curriculum research consultation. Beginning with the consultant and some of his problems, we moved to a consideration of the group as a whole, then to tensions within the group. The particular sequence of activities grew out of our needs as we progressed. The learnings became increasingly important as the semester went on. In an attempt to study the general growth of our perceptions, we analyzed the relation of our evaluation of each meeting to our awareness of what had been significant about the meeting.

In the pages that follow, three of the seminar projects are described, and an evaluation statement prepared by a seminar subcommittee and based on a two-hour recorded discussion is summarized.

Identifying Group Needs for Self-Training in Human Relations

One of the first problems we became aware of was our own weakness in the area of human relations. We talked about this problem for some time, but to get some facts about it we filled out an inventory called "Ideas about Myself," which was adapted from a similar instrument used at the 1950 National Training Laboratory for Group Development. This inventory consisted of forty-five items. Each item was responded to twice: first, to indicate "As I am" and second, "As I wish I were." Thus, item 14, "I often get so wound up in what I want to say that I don't really listen to what other people are saying," was checked twice by each member of the seminar according to the following response key:

⊕ A very accurate description of me
\+ Quite true as a description of me
? Both true and untrue of me
− Generally untrue of me
⊖ A decidedly false description of me

In the left margin we used a symbol that described our view of ourselves as we were, and in the right margin we used a symbol that described ourselves as we would like to be. These two self-ratings made it possible to compare our perception of our present behavior with our perceived goal, so far as certain aspects of group behavior were concerned. As a basis for comparison, we had available the responses of two groups of public school principals and curriculum coordinators to the same instrument.

We informally discussed, as a group, some tentative hypotheses that we expected would be supported by data from this inventory. We predicted, first, that we would tend to be more definite in our ideas of what we would like to be than in our perception of what we were. Second, we anticipated that because individual objectives or goals within the group were very much alike, the responses of seminar members to items on the inventory would show a great deal of similarity. With hypotheses like these in mind, a committee studied the evidence from the inventory.

Two different analyses were made of the data. The more exact method involved weighting each response and identifying those items on which the members of the seminar as a group expressed greatest dissatisfaction with themselves. The ten items that were identified by this method of analysis, in order of "dissatisfaction with self," are as follows:

1. I often get so wound up in what I want to say that I don't really listen to what other people are saying.
2. I am often tactless and hurt people's feelings without meaning to.

3. I am pretty good at finding ways to bring together two people who seem to be disagreeing.
4. I feel blocked and frustrated in my own school situation because of the difficulties resulting from the attitudes of certain people there.
5. I am aware of most of the shortcomings in my social behavior.
6. My relationships with other people never present much difficulty for me.
7. I would say I am more likely to dominate a group than to be dominated by it.
8. When someone is talking, I not only listen to what he says but also notice how people react to the things that he says.
9. I can usually predict the reactions of people whom I know to new suggestions.
10. I feel very much on the spot when people discuss faults that I know I have.

When the range and mean of the circled responses in the column "As I am" were compared with those in the column "As I wish I were," it was clear that we tended to be more definite in our ideas of what we would like to be than in our perception of what we were. The generalizations based on our responses to "Ideas about Myself" may be summarized as follows:

1. The areas in which we had the clearest differences of opinion involved group relationships and group roles.
2. Those areas in which we felt the most dissatisfaction with ourselves had to do with sensitivity to the feelings, thoughts, and ideas of people with whom we worked.
3. We were more definite in our ideas of what we would like to be than in our perception of what we were.
4. Those areas in which we felt the most satisfaction with ourselves as we were involved individuality and individual responsibility in a group.
5. Although each of us expressed a different degree of desire for improvement, the percentage of responses indi-

cating dissatisfaction was not very high for the group as a whole.

Practicing Sensitivity to Hurt Feelings

Our use of the "Ideas about Myself" instrument and our consideration of the barriers to effective educational consultation directed our attention to questions such as the following: "What is the effect on group work of the frequency with which feelings are hurt? . . . What kinds of situations seem to increase the tendency of people in the group to hurt one another? . . . What is an individual likely to do when his feelings are hurt? . . . What can be done to reduce the incidence of hurt feelings?"

Our interest in these questions developed as we discussed them. We were not interested primarily in an extensive analysis of the underlying reasons for sensitivity to hurt or a disposition to inflict hurt. Our concern was practical; we wanted to know more about what, if anything, a curriculum research consultant might do in a situation where feelings were being hurt.

After talking about this problem for a while, we decided that we needed some firsthand experience of hurtful situations. Consequently, we devoted two of the seminar periods to designing, conducting, and analyzing role-playing situations that we believed would give us the kind of practice we needed.

We undertook this task with the following tentatively formulated hypotheses in mind:
1. Role-playing will increase our sensitivity to actions that hurt.
2. We shall be able to agree fairly well in our identification of hurtful behavior.
3. We shall be able to formulate rather specific generalizations regarding the nature and dynamics of hurtful situations.

4. A repeated role-playing of the same situation, in which these generalizations are applied, will result in (*a*) fewer hurts and (*b*) greater progress on the problem being discussed.

Our over-all plan followed, in general, this sequence.

First, a concrete conflict situation, which one member of the seminar had recently experienced, was described and clarified for the group. The situation involved trouble in the cafeteria of a high school. Some of the boys and girls had gotten out of hand and had thrown milk cartons. The manager of the cafeteria felt seriously threatened. The children paid little attention to her requests for quiet and tidiness. The principal had for several days picked things up in the cafeteria, hoping that his example would affect the behavior of the boys and girls. The example was not followed. Certain members of the faculty were annoyed because, since they were assigned to supervise the cafeteria, much of the responsibility for the bedlam was placed on them. The high school was one in which the boys and girls, even though there was a student council, made no major decisions.

After a rather general description of the situation had been given, we spent some time establishing the temperament and character of the cafeteria manager, the high school principal, the chairman of the faculty advisory committee, and the faculty advisor to the student council. These were the persons who were to take part in the staff meeting called to consider the situation, and it was this staff meeting that we role-played.

Various members of the seminar group volunteered to play the roles. In addition, one of us acted as an "alter ego" for each of the role-players, with these specific instructions: "Do your best to identify (1) each time you believe your role-player is hurting another person and (2) each time some other person seems to be hurting your role-player." An attempt was made to note down enough about these situations to enable us to reconstruct them afterward. One member of the seminar tried independently to keep a record of all the hurts administered and received.

The role-playing situation lasted about fifteen minutes and was developed realistically. The cafeteria manager was anxious and frustrated. The chairman of the faculty committee blamed the children. The student council advisor defended the children and called attention to the fact that they rarely had a chance to make important decisions and that it was therefore unrealistic to expect them to take over the supervision of the cafeteria. The principal himself tried to evade responsibility whenever he could. No noticeable progress was made in formulating plans to improve the cafeteria.

At the end of the role-playing each of the "alter egos" interviewed his role-player in an attempt to achieve deeper insight into the dynamics of hurtful situations. After the interviewing and a general discussion, which went on for about an hour, we brought together the ideas concerning hurtful behavior that we felt had either been reinforced or suggested for the first time.

One of our hypotheses had been that we would be in substantial agreement in our perception of hurtful situations. Some test of this hypothesis, in respect to frequency, at least, is indicated by the following totals: estimates by "alter egos"—eighteen hurts intended and eleven received; estimates by over-all observer—twenty-three hurts intended and twenty-two received. This agreement was only fair, and we realized the necessity for clarifying what we meant by "hurts." We also realized that even when observers agreed that a hurt had been inflicted, the role-players themselves were frequently not aware that hurts had been directed at them.

The interviewing and discussion that followed the role-playing led to these generalizations:

A person is likely to be hurt when—
1. His convictions are rejected by other people in the group.
2. Any situation with which he is identified and for which he feels responsible is disparaged.
3. A situation he believes to be important and serious is not accepted as important and serious by others.
4. Others refuse to accept what he believes is their share of the blame and by implication place it all on him.
5. He reads criticisms or hostile feelings from the grimaces or ways of speaking or inflections of others.
6. His work or achievement or status is criticized, directly or indirectly.
7. He is anxious or insecure or feels unsafe, either because of his involvement in the problem under discussion or because of other situations that may not be brought into the discussion.
8. Someone else might not be bothered at all. There are great individual variations in susceptibility to hurt.
9. He has just hurt someone else.
10. Someone else has been hurt, but not necessarily by him.

We also gave some attention to what might be done to reduce the incidence of hurt feelings. We agreed that making it possible for individuals in a group to express frankly what their feelings are and why they feel threatened would tend to reduce their need to hurt one another. We also concluded that making it easier for members of a group to describe their insecurities would be beneficial. Finally, we decided that the spiral of a hurt given for a hurt received might be at least partially arrested if one or more members of the group decided to absorb some attacks without overt retaliation.

At the conclusion of this seminar session we decided that we would replay the same situation, with the same role-players, at our next meeting. We would assume that they had, in the meantime, taken part in a discussion of the effect of hurt feelings on a group's ability to solve problems. Because the person playing the role of the principal was absent, another member of the group volunteered to be the assistant principal, sent to the meeting by the principal. This changed the total situation somewhat. "Alter egos" for the role-players were again designated, and this time two people attempted to keep a record of all the hurts administered and received in order to increase the reliability of observation. Two other observers were selected. One person paid particular attention to the opportunities that the role-players had to practice the generalizations we thought might reduce the number of hurts. Another member of the group recorded specific applications of these three generalizations.

Again the role-playing lasted fifteen minutes. There was much less tension. A definite plan was about to be evolved when time was called. This fact was substantiated in the interviews following the role-playing. Interpersonal feelings were appreciably better than in the first role-playing situation. We were unable, however, to analyze reasons for this to our complete satisfaction because the assistant principal played a role noticeably different from that played by the principal in the first session.

After the role-playing had been completed, we spent about an hour discussing our observations, interviewing the role-players, and comparing our records of hurts administered and received. We found that it was difficult to put into practice, in a dynamic situation, the generalizations we had reached regarding ways to reduce the incidence of hurts. Although we kept these generalizations in mind, we found that they were difficult to put into operation even in a role-playing situation.

Our tallies showed that there were substantially fewer hurts administered and received during the second role-playing situation than during the first. The reasons were probably various, but we felt our fourth hypothesis (see p. 114) had been supported. There was general agreement, too, among all the observers and role-players, that greater progress on the problem—that is, how to improve the cafeteria—was made during the second role-playing situation than during the first.

Evaluating the Seminar Sessions

At the end of each seminar session we rated the meeting on a five-point scale. A score of 5 indicated the highest possible rating (excellent), 3 represented a mediocre rating (so-so), and 1 represented the lowest rating (very poor). Next to the numerical rating we wrote whatever comments about the meeting seemed pertinent to us. Typically, these comments had to do with the reasons for assigning a particular rating to a meeting. Average ratings and the range of ratings were calculated for each meeting. These ratings, or post-seminar evaluations, were reported to the group at the end of each session.

The hypothesis underlying this seminar activity was as follows: There is a relationship between the ratings given to a meeting and the tendency of group members to discuss certain elements of the meeting. The following assumptions were made in interpreting the data:

1. The rating assigned to a meeting is a valid indication of the general feeling of the rater about the meeting.
2. The comments made by the rater give a valid indication of what he considers significant about the meeting.

Using the post-seminar evaluations, we attempted to determine what relationships, if any, existed between the average ratings given to a meeting and the elements of the meeting considered significant by members of the group. These relationships were not thought of necessarily as cause-and-effect relationships.

There was some fluctuation in the average ratings given to the meetings between February 8 and March 1. After March 8 there was a relatively steady slight improvement in the ratings given to the meetings. An analysis of comments made on the post-seminar evaluations of these later meetings indicated that the following elements were discussed: the content, the way the chairman worked, the number of people who participated, the way consensus on ideas and action proposals was gained, the ability to form and adhere to an agenda, and the general feeling-tone, or atmosphere, of the meetings. Comments concerning these matters were tabulated for each meeting. The tabulation did not indicate whether a comment was favorable or unfavorable; it indicated only the particular element of group work to which the comment referred. The fact that an element was named was taken as an indication that it was perceived as important. The reverse, of course, would not be true.

The following relationships between the kinds of elements mentioned and the post-seminar evaluations seemed to exist:

1. The last three meetings included in this report received high ratings. These meetings received proportionately more comments on the content of the meeting than meetings to which lower ratings were given.
2. High ratings of meetings were accompanied by considerable comment on participation. Only one of the meetings that was given a high rating did not receive this kind of comment. The two meetings rated lowest received very few comments on participation.
3. No relationship was apparent between statements about feeling-tone and ratings given to meetings.

The most significant relationship found was that between high ratings and comments on the content of the meetings. The fact that the high average ratings tended to cluster at the end of the eleven-meeting period suggests that the group had reached sufficient maturity by then to give relatively more attention to content and less to process. High ratings were associated with a feeling that objective progress was being made, and with a reduction of concern about the mechanics of group work. It is interesting, for example, that there were very few comments about the chairman's conduct of the meeting during the last three seminar sessions; previously there had been considerable comment on his role. Similarly, there was relatively little comment on the ability to adhere to an agenda during the last three meetings; previously this had called for substantially more comment. References to the achievement of consensus followed the same general pattern.

Evaluating the Seminar as a Whole

In an attempt to review how we had handled our problems, we devoted the final two-hour session of the seminar to an evaluation discussion. This discussion was recorded on tape and analyzed by a subcommittee. The generalizations and comments that resulted from the analysis are presented here.

1. We realized that our learnings were tentative and required further testing and consolidation.

For example, we agreed that increased sensitivity to the need for changing our behavior did not in itself give assurance that we would be able to act in the desired fashion. One member testified to her failure, in a number of situations similar to those we had been studying, to respond quickly enough to be very effective.

Another member reported an experience she had had, which was very much like one of the practice sessions. A teacher had come up to her, in the hallway of one of the schools where she was gaining field experience, with the question, "Now what do you think of your progressive education?" The seminar member recognized this as a challenge but did not know what the teacher really had in mind. A brief, rather nondirective conversation revealed that the teacher had meant to blame progressive education for what seemed to her to be undue noise in the corridor. Although unable, because of lack of time, to continue the discussion, the student then applied what the group thought it had learned in a training session. She agreed with the teacher that undue noise or lack of discipline was something about which everyone should be concerned. The learnings involved in this situation were (*a*) guarding against defensiveness under apparent attack; (*b*) searching for meaning underneath the emotional tone of a challenge; and (*c*) finding something of significance for joint consideration.

The inference we drew from examples such as these was that the ability to apply the sensitivity acquired in group training sessions required separate practice. This conclusion suggested that an extension of seminar time, to be used, perhaps, for laboratory sessions, was needed. It also suggested the need for considering learnings as tentative and subject to testing and development in real situations. This need might not be eliminated even with further training in a protected group situation.

2. We regarded field situations as a source of problems for training sessions and as a testing ground for our learnings.

The relationship of field situations to the seminar, somewhat vague at first, became clarified for us as we went along. Most of us were engaged, as part of our seminar activity, in curriculum work in the field. We found that this field activity determined a great deal of what went on in the seminar. We concluded, too, that the learnings from the seminar received their most effective testing in the field. For example, one of us was called upon in a school situation to react to a lengthy statement in which the speaker was personally involved. He used the technique of summarizing as developed in one of our sessions and found it effective in moving the group ahead without losing the "involved" member.

The seminar provided opportunities for learning human relations concepts, attitudes, and skills under circumstances that did not imply "playing for keeps." The permissive atmosphere we were able to develop not only condoned mistakes but enabled us to use them in a fruitful way. We concluded that, having experienced some of the skills and satisfactions of a group's growing through self-analysis, we would be more likely to see the same possibilities in future group work in the field.

3. *The design of our action research grew out of our own activity.*

Although we were intellectually aware of the action research pattern when the seminar started, we did not consciously impose it on ourselves at the outset. Instead, our research pattern grew out of the apparent strengths and weaknesses of our way of working. For example, we became aware of the need for skepticism regarding any generalizations about social behavior. This skepticism resulted in part from the difficulty of obtaining pertinent evidence. Our evidence was sometimes scattered and fragmentary, and less than adequate to support valid conclusions. Therefore we tried to set up additional test situations that would provide a greater quantity of reliable data. We also tried to document and analyze data in a manner that would yield tenable conclusions.

Our pattern of research, then, was to formulate a tentative hypothesis, provide ourselves with a common experience that would offer an opportunity to collect evidence, discuss the evidence, restate the hypothesis in the light of new understandings, provide ourselves with additional experience to test the new hypothesis, and so on. As we attained greater discipline in research techniques, we felt a growing satisfaction about seminar activities.

4. Probably we are more cautious about attributing feelings and meanings to others than we were before we had these training sessions. Certainly we are more aware of the influence our own feelings have on our relationships with others.

We are continuously engaged in judging the feelings of others, interpreting what they say or do, or predicting how they will react. These activities are the essence of communication. We make judgments, interpretations, or predictions about others at all levels of our acquaintance with them. One important basis for our success in relating ourselves to our fellow-workers is the extent to which we understand how they feel and what they are trying to say.

We realized that we had been far too ready to jump to conclusions about the feelings and meanings of others. Our experience in trying to determine how others feel, particularly in the series of sessions on hurtful behavior, taught us how difficult the job is. Our weekly post-meeting reactions to seminar sessions frequently indicated how varied a response the same experience could arouse. In our attempts to evaluate the insights we were gaining from training experiences that we had designed together, we were frequently impressed with the differences in the perceptions of group members. Moreover, we came to see with greater clarity how much we tended to read our own thoughts and feelings into what others were saying.

We have become more fully aware of the need for examining our own feelings, especially under conditions of strain. We think we are better able to account for the reactions we have to what others say or do or mean as a result of what we believe to be their intentions toward us. For example, we think we now understand better the part that defense of official status may play in some of the attacks made upon us. We also have gained some awareness of how the need to defend our own status may influence our tenddency to perceive hostility in others. We consider ourselves more sensitive to the overtones of feeling that accompany our own statements as well as those of others.

Knowledge of how people *really* feel and what they *really* mean became central to our development. The training sessions contributed to our awareness that gaining such knowledge is very difficult. And, perhaps more fully than before, we realize the importance of the search for reliable evidence concerning feelings and meanings.

5. *Such success as we have had in training ourselves for curriculum consultation through action research has come because the research was planned in and by and for the group.*

Using ourselves individually as a source of needs, through the instrument "Ideas about Myself," we pooled our expressions of concern and went to work to increase our skills and understandings. Once we had found common problems, we decided to concentrate on improvement of group insights. We decided, when the issue was raised, to keep the focus on the group rather than turn to what the experience was doing to and for individuals. We felt less threat in this emphasis. We also believed that group analysis and group training would provide an excellent environment for individual improvement.

We believe that the greater length of time we spent on each succeeding phase of our training experience indicates that we became increasingly able, during the course of the semester, to carry out group purposes. We returned once to our original problem finding device to see what progress we were making toward common goals. We tried to involve the entire group in discussions and analyses of work done by special subcommittees because we were somewhat uneasy about the functioning of these committees apart from the larger body. We felt that all of us should participate in the major creative activities of the seminar.

Our best use of action research as a seminar learning method was illustrated by our study of hurtful behavior, which has been described earlier in this chapter. First, we took sufficient time to define our problem carefully, and obtained data that helped in the definition process. Second, we formulated several action hypotheses and worked out a design for testing them in the seminar situation. Third, we realized that we needed a certain kind of evidence for the testing, and we devised ways of getting this evidence. Fourth, after studying the evidence as well as our entire procedure, we formulated conclusions carefully. Finally, all members of the group were actively involved throughout the research process. Everyone made his talents available to all the others. The inquiry was genuinely cooperative.

CHAPTER VII

Action Research, Statistics and the Sampling Problem

One of the best ways of discouraging classroom teachers or other practical school people from experimenting is to emphasize statistics as such. This is quite different from emphasizing the value of getting maximum meaning from quantitative data. It is almost impossible to do the latter without learning some statistical concepts and operations. When a teacher—or anyone else, for that matter—needs precise, quantitative measures of central tendency or variability or the relationship among variables in order to understand something he wants very much to understand, statistics take on a surprisingly different significance.

The Effect of Courses in Statistics

Many of the school people with whom members of the Institute staff work as action research consultants have a Master's degree in education. Most of them have taken a graduate course in educational statistics or educational measurement. Usually, however, they have learned little from these courses that helps them do their work more effectively.

This generalization is based not only on testimony willingly given by these teachers but also on the way they first work with quantitative data when they are conducting their own action research studies. They undoubtedly acquired some facility in talking about statistical concepts and operations while taking the course, but rarely did this facility enable them to use statistics later.

There probably are a number of reasons why courses in educational statistics are viewed by practical school people as contributing but slightly if at all to their professional growth. The courses seem to have at least two basic weaknesses. The first is that the exercises and problems used are so remote from the needs and interests of educational practitioners that the experience is almost meaningless. The following example, only slightly adapted from one actually found in several widely used texts, illustrates this point:

> Plot two frequency polygons of the 100 scores given on p. —, using intervals of 3 and of 5 units. Note that these are continuous data. Smooth these distributions (see p. —) and superimpose histograms.

It is not difficult to understand the motivation of a teacher of English, social studies, science, or foreign language, or that of a supervisor or principal, who performed all the operations necessary for completing this exercise. The warning, "Note that these are continuous data," is especially interesting. In one text several pages are devoted to the various procedures for establishing class interval limits in frequency tables of continuous data.

Here is another exercise, again only slightly paraphrased, which at first glance, given the nature of the data, seems to be most practical. Solving this problem might interest teachers who have become intrigued with statistics as such, but it is doubtful whether many instructors of statistics courses take so much trouble with the grades they assign.

Letter grades are assigned by three teachers of Latin, three teachers of algebra, and three teachers of home economics, as follows:

Grade	Latin	Algebra	Home Economics
A	26	10	5
B	20	26	16
C	31	19	24
D	0	7	19
F	4	3	7
Total grades	81	65	71

 a. Express each distribution in per cents and change these per cents into standard scores.
 b. Change these standard scores into two-digit numbers and into Z-scores.
 c. Find the average grades for these students:

Student	Latin	Algebra	Home Economics
SH	A	B	C
FM	C	B	A
DB	B	D	F

The second weakness of much statistical instruction for classroom teachers is that an attempt is made to teach too much. For anyone who likes arithmetic and algebra and has an inkling of the calculus, a concentrated course in educational statistics can be fascinating. Such people, however, constitute but a small group in the typical required statistics course.

The observation that the usual one-semester course in educational statistics, even on the graduate level, tries to teach too much too quickly is supported by even a casual examination of the table of contents of any one of the widely used texts. The classroom teacher, supervisor, or administrator will receive little help in improving his practices from spending hours on the calculation of the mean or standard deviation by the "short" method (approximately nine pages); practicing the use of sampling formulas (approximately ten pages); computing indices of curvilinear relationship (about seventeen pages); or understanding the Wheery-Doolittle test-selection method (eighteen separate steps and about sixteen pages). This contention is not intended as a criticism of texts dealing so extensively with these operations; rather, it is a criticism of placing the operations very high on the list of understandings and skills that practical school people need in order to study their problems more scientifically.

Most educational practitioners report not only that the usual introductory course in statistics helps them little in their own investigations but also that it helps them little if at all in their attempts to read research reports written by others. The validity of this generalization will have to be supported or rejected by the experience of those readers who have had a single course in educational statistics and have subsequently tried to use what they learned as a basis for criticizing reports of educational investigations. There is some objective evidence of the unfavorable reaction of practicing school people to their graduate courses in statistics and educational measurement, which are usually remembered as having contributed little to professional growth. This is a problem of real concern to teachers of statistics courses. At one major institution offering graduate work to many supervisors and curriculum coordinators, the content of a course in statistics is being planned so that the course will be of maximum usefulness to this special group.

In my own work with teachers and others who actually are engaged in action research, two generalizations about the role of statistics have impressed me most strongly. The first is that when it becomes necessary for school people to learn how to treat quantitative data in order to answer questions in which they are genuinely interested, the learning of statistics goes rapidly. In other words, when the ability to compute and use statistical indices is a means to an important end, it is not resisted. The second generalization is that familiarity with just a few of the basic statistical concepts and operations is sufficient to help the action researcher study his problems more scientifically.

Statistical Concepts and Operations for Experimenting Teachers

In the great majority of investigations undertaken by teachers or other practical school people to enable them to do their jobs more adequately, the statistical concepts that are most helpful are relatively simple. This has proved to be true in most of the cooperative studies with which members of the Horace Mann-Lincoln Institute staff have been associated. One concept has to do with a measure of central tendency. The common index of central tendency is either the mean or the median. The latter is easily arrived at by arranging scores in sequence of magnitude and identifying the middle one or averaging the middle two. When it is necessary to find a mean, or average, this is usually done with least trouble by the so-called long method. The "long" method is, after all, not very long if one is working with thirty or thirty-five scores. Some statistician should calculate how much time is wasted by finding an average by the "short" method for relatively small populations.

The need for a measure of central tendency when examining experimental evidence is clear. Recognition of the importance of taking into account variability, or spread, comes with more difficulty. In working with teachers or others engaged in action research, variability of scores is best approached by a consideration of range. There are almost always available from studies conducted by the teachers themselves meaningful data illustrating that the range of scores may differ appreciably from group to group even though the central tendency is about the same. It is not difficult to see that this phenomenon has interesting and significant implications for teaching. From the consideration of range it is an easy step to a realization that one extreme score at either end of the distribution distorts the range appreciably. A more stable measure of variability, and one that is useful for most of the purposes of experimenting teachers, is the interquartile range. This is the distance between the top fourth and the bottom fourth of the scores when they are arranged in order of magnitude. A more conventional measure is the semi-interquartile range, which is this same value divided by two.

Until teachers develop an interest in statistical analysis for its own sake or wish to make relatively unusual interpretations of their data, they have little use for the standard deviation. To get the difference between each score and the mean, square these differences, get their average, and then extract the square root of this average, seems to a teacher to be a roundabout way to find out about variability. And it is, if variability is all one is interested in. The fact that the standard deviation is necessary for any use of formulas dealing with sampling errors is usually not relevant.

Of the more complicated statistical concepts, those having to do with correlation almost always receive a great deal of attention in action research studies. Teachers trying to get maximum meaning from their experimental data are interested in the interrelationship among variables. In most instances the number of cases involved warrants the use of a simple formula, such as the one used to get rank correlation.[1] Even this formula looks complicated to many teachers, but with a little practice they are able to compute their own coefficients. When these correlations suggest interesting interpretations of their data, the teachers usually feel repaid for their efforts.

Just what meaning to ascribe to a coefficient of correlation based on thirty cases is, of course, problematical. It is necessary to help beginning action researchers to understand how large a correlation coefficient may be obtained through the operation of chance factors only. Actually computing some chance correlations involving twenty-five or thirty cases is interesting and dramatically enlightening. A simple way of doing this is to number two packs of cards from 1 to 30 and to consider these numbers as ranks. Each pile is then shuffled, and correlations are computed between the chance relationships. To spend an hour with a group of teachers on this kind of computation helps them to realize that correlations of considerable magnitude may be the result of chance factors.

There are times, of course, when it is inadvisable to use the rank method of correlation. In that case it is helpful to think of the coefficient of correlation as the average of the standard-score cross-products. This is the basic concept of the product moment coefficient, and all formulas are derived from it algebraically. A teacher can determine the standard score for each pupil in respect to two variables, multiply these standard scores, sum them, get their average, and come out with a highly respectable product moment coefficient of correlation.

Teachers who are experimenting with more promising methods, materials, or class groupings are willing and sometimes even eager to learn methods of statistical analysis that they see they must learn in order to get answers to their own questions. They do not, however, want to do what seems to them analogous to using a micrometer for measuring pieces of wood for a rustic bench.

Action Research and the Sampling Problem[*]

Problems of population sampling do not very often arise in action research undertaken by practical school people be-

[*] The material on p. 132-139 was included in "Action Research by Teachers and the Population Sampling Problem," which appeared in *The Journal of Educational Psychology*, 43:331-338, October 1952.

cause teachers usually experiment with the total population in which they are especially interested. When teachers begin to wonder to what extent the generalizations resulting from a particular experiment are applicable to pupils they may have in the future, it is possible to develop quite a bit of interest in sampling theory.

Action research is sometimes criticized because its findings are not necessarily applicable to other school systems or to school children in other school systems. The reason for this criticism is that the boys and girls or teachers who are the subjects of the action research do not represent a random, or representative, sample of boys and girls or teachers in other school systems. This fact precludes extending the generalizations from action research studies to populations that have not been randomly sampled in the studies. Teachers, supervisors, and administrators in a given school system can with confidence put into practice the generalizations resulting from action research conducted in other school systems only when the populations about which they are concerned are similar to those on which the action research was based. An alternative and common-sense justification for using what action research has revealed to be desirable in other situations is the subjective conviction, based on the report of the action research itself, that one's own situation and that in which the inquiry was conducted are strikingly alike.

Generalizing from Action Research

The problem of population sampling that must be faced by people engaged in action research is implied by the nature of this kind of inquiry. If a teacher in the third grade of a particular school conducts action research, he usually does so for two reasons. First, he wants to make better decisions and engage in better practices *now*. Second, he hopes that the generalizations that apply to his present pupils will apply also to the boys and girls he will teach later. The degree to which the generalizations from his action research studies in 1953 are applicable to future groups of his pupils in the same class and school depends on the extent to which his present pupils represent a random sample of the cumulative population of children he will teach in the future.

This implies that action researchers are bound by the same canons about generalizing as investigators who engage in traditional educational research. The difference is that action research generalizations are to be extended in a different direction. The investigator who conducts a traditional inquiry using a random sampling of all the third grades in the state of Iowa or New York designs his study so that he will know the extent to which his generalizations are laterally applicable—applicable to all other third grades. The teacher engaged in action research, on the other hand, is concerned with the extent to which his generalizations can be extended vertically—into the future—and serve as guides for decisions and actions involving third-grade boys and girls he will teach but has not yet seen.

Testing the Hypothesis

Whether or not generalizations from investigations undertaken by a teacher to provide a better basis for decisions and actions concerning his present pupils can be extended to his future pupils in the same school and at the same grade level depends on the extent to which the following hypothesis can be supported:

> Boys and girls in a teacher's present class constitute a random, or representative, sample of the cumulative population of his future classes.

An analogous hypothesis, referring to present and future populations of teachers, PTA's, or any other group in a specific locality, could of course be formulated.

In the remainder of this chapter several tests of the hypothesis that a teacher's present class can be thought of as a random sample of the total population of his future classes are reported. The major steps involved in the computations are listed here.

1. A critical variable for which test scores were available was selected. The scores of all pupils taught by the same teacher at the same grade level for a series of several consecutive years were placed in a frequency table.
2. The frequencies in each class interval were expressed as percentages of the total cumulated population.
3. A frequency table of the scores for the critical variable was made for each of the separate classes. The same class intervals as those used for the total population were used in these tables.
4. The class frequencies were used as observed data, and their distribution was compared with the theoretical, or expected, distribution resulting from multiplying the frequency in each interval for a single class by the interval percentage established for the total population (see 2 above).
5. The chi-square test was applied to the null hypothesis that the distribution of scores in the individual classes and the distribution for the total population of N classes differed no more than might be expected as a consequence of chance or random factors.

The following illustration, involving the IQ's of three consecutive eighth-grade classes taught by a teacher in New York City,[2] may serve to clarify how these computations were actually carried out.

The total N for the three classes was 96. Table 1 represents a frequency distribution of the 96 IQ's. The last column gives the percentage of the total number of cases falling in each class interval.

TABLE 1

FREQUENCY DISTRIBUTION OF IQ'S FOR TOTAL POPULATION OF THREE CONSECUTIVE CLASSES

IQ Interval	f	Per cent
50– 69	1	1.0
70– 89	16	17.5
90–109	43	44.8
110–129	26	27.1
130–149	10	10.4

The first two columns of Table 2 shows a frequency distribution of IQ's for one of the classes. The class intervals used are identical with those used for the total population. The third column shows the expected, or theoretical, frequencies derived from multiplying the N for this particular class, 33, by the percentages in the last column of Table 1. The last three columns show the results of calculations necessary for determining chi-square, which in this case was 2.77.[3] With four degrees of freedom, P becomes 60, which means that in 60 per cent of a large number of trials we would expect the distribution of IQ's for a single class to differ *by chance* from the distribution of IQ's for the total population by at least as much as the observed differences (fo-fe).

TABLE 2

CHI-SQUARE TEST APPLIED TO DIFFERENCES BETWEEN FREQUENCY DISTRIBUTION OF IQ'S FOR A SINGLE CLASS AND FOR TOTAL POPULATION

IQ Interval	Observed f	Expected f	fo-fe	(fo-fe)²	$\frac{(fo\text{-}fe)^2}{fe}$
50– 69	1	.3	.7	.49	1.63
70– 89	4	5.8	1.8	3.24	.56
90–109	14	14.8	.8	.64	.04
110–129	11	8.9	2.1	4.41	.49
130–149	3	3.4	.4	.16	.05

The interpretation, then, is that the null hypothesis cannot be rejected. So far as IQ's are concerned, this single class can be considered a chance, or random, sample of the total three-class population.

All in all, 38 similar chi-squares were computed. Pupils in twelve different class sequences taught by twelve teachers in New York City and West Orange, New Jersey, were the subjects of the analysis; and the variables were IQ's, subject-matter achievement test scores, and silent reading test scores.

The first test of the hypothesis involved the IQ's of twenty-seven eighth-grade classes taught by nine New York City teachers. (Nine sequences of three consecutive classes, each sequence taught by the same teacher, were used.) Table 3 shows a frequency distribution of P's for the 27 tests of the null hypothesis.

TABLE 3

P's for Tests of Null Hypothesis Applied to IQ's of Eighth-Grade New York City Pupils

P-Range	f
80–99	13
60–79	4
40–59	5
20–39	4
0–19	1

The second test of the hypothesis involved scores on the Iowa Silent Reading Test for three consecutive seventh-grade classes taught by a teacher in West Orange, New Jersey, and four consecutive tenth-grade classes taught by another teacher in that community. The number of chi-squares possible to compute was 7, and the P's were all in excess of 5, which again indicated that rejection of the null hypothesis was not warranted.

The third test involved Standard test scores on the Language Arts and Arithmetic parts of the Stanford Achievement Test for four consecutive sixth-grade classes taught by a West Orange, New Jersey, teacher. All the chi-squares were equal to or smaller than the number of degrees of freedom, and the P's were 71, 53, 53, and 40.

Table 4 summarizes the P's resulting from all 38 chi-square tests of the null hypothesis. With the possible exception of one ($P = 7$), all implied that it would be hazardous to reject the hypothesis that the pupils in a teacher's class at any one time can, so far as the variables dealt with here are concerned, be considered a random sample of a total population of several consecutive classes.

TABLE 4

CHI-SQUARE P'S RESULTING FROM
38 TESTS OF NULL HYPOTHESIS

P-Range	f
80–99	14
60–79	7
40–59	10
20–39	5
0–19	2

Conclusion

The null hypothesis that the distribution of scores in a single class would not be substantially different from the distribution of scores in a series of classes taught by the same teacher was supported in all but one instance. The only criterion used to obtain these test cases was the availability of scores over a period of years. It is conceivable that the pupil populations in a school might change so radically under some circumstances that no given population for one year could be considered a random sample of a total population enrolled in the school over a period of years. It is also conceivable that small increments of change, which are not appreciable for a three- or four-year period, might become so over a longer period. Nevertheless, the analyses reported in this chapter provide considerable support for extending, within the limits suggested by conventional formulas based on assumptions of random sampling, generalizations derived from action research studies of a teacher's present class to at least several immediately following classes.

NOTES TO

CHAPTER VII

1. This formula is as follows:

$$R = 1 - \frac{6\Sigma d^2}{N(N^2-1)}$$

with d representing the difference between the two ranks given to the same individual, and N, the number of persons or items ranked. Σ means "the sum of." $6\Sigma d^2$ is six times the sum of all the differences in rank squared.

2. I am indebted to J. Wayne Wrightstone for providing the New York City scores, and to Ronald C. Doll for the West Orange, New Jersey, scores.

3. The correction for continuity (see H. E. Garrett, *Statistics in Psychology and Education* [New York, Longmans, Green and Company, 1947], p. 246 f.) was not applied to these chi-squares, in spite of the small number of entries in some of the class intervals, because the uncorrected chi-square is a more rigorous test of the null hypothesis. The latter was supported in all but one instance despite this added rigor.

CHAPTER VIII

In Summary

Action research in education is research undertaken by practitioners in order that they may improve their practices. The people who actually teach children, supervise teachers, or administer school systems attempt to solve their practical problems by using the methods of science. They accumulate evidence to define their problems more sharply. They draw on all of the experience available to them for action hypotheses that give promise of enabling them to ameliorate or eliminate the difficulties of their day-to-day work. They test out these promising procedures on the job and accumulate evidence of their effectiveness. They try to generalize as carefully as possible in order that their research may contribute to the solution of future problems or to the elimination of future difficulties.

One of the psychological values of action research is that the people who must, by the very nature of their professional responsibilities, improve their practices are the ones who engage in the research to learn what represents improvement. They themselves try out new and seemingly more promising ways of teaching or supervising or administering, and they study the consequences.

There are two alternatives to action research as a method

of improving educational practices. One, a procedure that most people resort to as they try to do their jobs more adequately, is to make changes on the basis of subjective impressions of what the problems are. Then, with a minimum of emphasis on testing or the accumulation of objective evidence, judgments are formed about the consequences of the attempted improvements.

The second alternative is to ask the professional educational investigator to study the problems and suggest solutions. This alternative has two basic limitations. In the first place, the professional investigator can never study individual problems in any strict sense. They are peculiar to the particular situation and people involved. A second limitation is that even when the recommendations are sound, it is difficult to incorporate them into the behavior patterns of practitioners. It is relatively easy to talk a better kind of teaching or supervising or administering as a consequence of reading or hearing what others say should be done. But there is a great difference between this modification in vocabulary and any substantial modification in behavior. An indispensable part of action research is actual practice of more promising procedures.

Probably the major difference between action research and traditional educational research arises from the motivation of the investigators. In fundamental research the basic aim is to conduct an inquiry that will result in generalizations of broad applicability. The traditional educational researcher is motivated by his desire to arrive at "the truth." If he is cautious, he will report findings as "true" only within certain limits of probability. But to the degree that the investigation results in generalizations of the widest possible applicability, it is considered to be excellent research.

Those who engage in action research do so primarily because they wish to improve their own practices. Action research is conducted in the heat of combat, so to speak.

It is conducted by teachers or supervisors or administrators in order that they may know, on the basis of relatively objective evidence, whether or not they are accomplishing the things they hope to accomplish.

The differences in methodology between traditional research and action research are minor. Each investigator attempts to define the problem being studied with precision, to derive his hypotheses from as rich a background of information related to the problem as possible, to design an inquiry so that it will result in a genuine test of the hypotheses, to use facts or evidence rather than subjective impressions throughout the research procedure, and to generalize cautiously and tentatively from the evidence collected. The conditions under which the two investigators carry out their inquiries, however, may differ appreciably. The traditional investigator in education tries to control a situation so that many of the variables involved in real teaching or supervising or administering are ruled out by definition or by the use of laboratory techniques. This practice results in a more definitive test of the stated hypotheses. But precision is gained at the expense of the relevance of the findings. People engaged in action research conduct their inquiries in the complicated psycho-sociological climate of on-going school activities. Because of the multiplicity of variables involved, the research is often lacking in precision. The results, however, have meaning for practice because they derive from an inquiry carried out in a real situation.

A dominant theme in the argument of this book has been that research quality must be viewed in relative terms. It is possible to progress gradually from the casual method ordinarily used to cope with practical difficulties to a method much more scrupulously scientific. As improvements are made in the methodology of action research, increased confidence in the inferences and generalizations drawn from the research data becomes possible.

Improvements in method can characterize any element of the total process of research. To expect to leap all at once from the everyday method of common sense to a method that incorporates the best scientific procedures is unrealistic. But to improve gradually requires little more than a commitment to the method of science and a willingness to take the chances that are always involved in experimentation. A commitment to the method of science is more likely to result from the persuasion of events than from the persuasion of other men. Relatively dependable consequences are available only when the scientific method is used. It is this dependability of results that argues most strongly for the scientific method of problem solving—for action research. The best way of learning how to conduct action research and of discovering the values it possesses is to try it.

Action research in the field of education need not involve the cooperative activities of a number of people, but in most instances cooperation is highly desirable. Many of the improvements that should be made in teaching, supervising, or administering cannot be effected if only one person changes his behavior. Little can be done about most important educational difficulties unless a number of people modify their ideas and practices. Therefore, as many as possible of the people who will be affected by attempts to improve a difficult situation should be involved in those attempts. The cooperative efforts of all these people will tend to result in better problem definition, more realistic consideration of action hypotheses, easier translation of these hypotheses into action, and better interpretation of the evidence accumulated, than the efforts of any one of them alone.

Making action research cooperative introduces all the complications involved in group work. If cooperative action research is to be most effective, members of working groups must feel free to introduce modifications in their procedures.

Their ways of working must be appropriate to the job they are working on, and they must have numerous opportunities to try out and evaluate processes that give promise of increasing productivity.

If the quality of the methods now being employed by teachers, supervisors, and administrators in attacking their problems is to improve, there must be a considerable change in the working environment and atmosphere of most school systems. Whether or not these changes will be effected, whether or not conditions favorable to action research will be established, depends largely on the status leaders. They must take the initiative in making it possible for teachers to admit and discuss their professional limitations, to hypothesize creatively, to have the resources and consultative help they need, to obtain the best possible evidence of the consequences of changes, and to derive from this evidence generalizations that are sound and helpful guides to future behavior.

Most of this book has been addressed to the status leaders in on-going school situations. The discussion of factors conducive to action research, and most of the illustrations, have been based on real schools or school systems. The clearest implications of action research are for in-service education. The theory of learning that results in action research suggests, however, a number of modifications in the pre-service education of teachers. They too should have numerous opportunities to conduct their own action research inquiries, as individuals and as members of a group. This implies that young people in pre-service training for teaching must accept greater responsibility for their own learning than they now do. It also implies that less emphasis should be placed on courses that require them to spend most of their time reading about, or listening to, what other people say they should do.

BIBLIOGRAPHY

Bibliography

1. ANDERSON, G. LESTER, and GATES, ARTHUR I. "The General Nature of Learning." National Society for the Study of Education. *Learning and Instruction.* Forty-ninth Yearbook, Part I. Chicago, University of Chicago Press, 1950. p. 12-35.
2. BANKS, TRESSA, FARLEY, EDGAR S., POWERS, OSCAR, VANDERMEER, FLOYD, WALDORF, ROBERT, and COREY, STEPHEN M. "We Tested Some Beliefs about the Biographical Method." *The School Review,* 59:157-163, March 1951.
3. BENNE, KENNETH D., and MUNTYAN, BOZIDAR. *Human Relations in Curriculum Change.* New York, The Dryden Press, c1951. 363 p.
4. BENNE, KENNETH D., and SHEATS, PAUL. "Functional Roles of Group Members." *The Journal of Social Issues,* 4:41-49, Spring 1948.
5. BENNE, KENNETH D., AXTELLE, GEORGE A., SMITH, B. OTHANEL, and RAUP, BRUCE. *The Discipline of Practical Judgment in a Democratic Society.* National Society of College Teachers of Education. Twenty-eighth Yearbook. Chicago, University of Chicago Press, 1943. 268 p.
6. BORING, EDWIN G. *A History of Experimental Psychology.* New York, The Century Company, c1929. 699 p.
7. BRADFORD, LELAND P. "The Case of the Hidden Agenda." *Adult Leadership,* 1:3-7, September 1952.
8. BUCKINGHAM, BURDETTE ROSS. *Research for Teachers.* New York, Silver, Burdett and Company, 1926. 386 p.

9. CAMPBELL, CLYDE M., ed. *Practical Applications of Democratic Administration.* New York, Harper and Brothers, c1952. 325 p.
10. CARTWRIGHT, DORWIN. "Achieving Change in People: Some Applications of Group Dynamics Theory." *Human Relations,* 4, no. 4:381-392, 1951.
11. CASWELL, HOLLIS L. "Research in the Curriculum." *Educational Leadership,* 7:438-445, April 1950.
12. CASWELL, HOLLIS L., and ASSOCIATES. *Curriculum Improvement in Public School Systems.* New York, Bureau of Publications, Teachers College, Columbia University, 1950. 462 p.
13. CHAMBERLAIN, DEAN, CHAMBERLAIN, ENID, DROUGHT, NEAL E., and SCOTT, WILLIAM E. *Did They Succeed in College?* New York, Harper and Brothers, c1942. 291 p.
14. CHAMBERS, WHITTAKER. *Witness.* New York, Random House, 1952. 808 p.
15. CHEIN, ISIDOR, COOK, STUART W., and HARDING, JOHN. "The Field of Action Research." *The American Psychologist,* 3:43-50, February 1948.
16. CHEIN, ISIDOR, COOK, STUART W., and HARDING, JOHN. "The Use of Research in Social Therapy." *Human Relations,* 1, no. 4:497-511, 1948.
17. COFFMAN, WILLIAM E. "Teacher Morale and Curriculum Development: A Statistical Analysis of Responses to a Reaction Inventory." *Journal of Experimental Education,* 19:305-332, June 1951.
18. COLLIER, JOHN. "United States Indian Administration as a Laboratory of Ethnic Relations." *Social Research,* 12:265-303, May 1945.
19. COMMITTEE ON OPERATIONS RESEARCH. "Operations Research with Special Reference to Non-military Operations." Washington, D. C., National Research Council, April 1951. 12 p.
20. COREY, STEPHEN M. "Action Research, Fundamental Research, and Educational Practices." *Teachers College Record,* 50:509-514, May 1949.
21. COREY, STEPHEN M. "Action Research by Teachers and the Population Sampling Problem." *The Journal of Educational Psychology,* 43:331-338, October 1952.
22. COREY, STEPHEN M. "Conditions Conducive to Curricular Experimentation." *Educational Administration and Supervision,* 36:209-216, April 1950.

23. COREY, STEPHEN M. "Curriculum Development through Action Research." *Educational Leadership*, 7:147-153, December 1949.
24. COREY, STEPHEN M. "Educational Research and the Solution of Practical Problems." *Educational Leadership*, 9:478-484, May 1952.
25. COREY, STEPHEN M. "An Experiment in Leadership Training." *Educational Administration and Supervision*, 37:321-328, October 1951.
26. COREY, STEPHEN M., FOSHAY, A. WELLESLEY, and MACKENZIE, GORDON N. "Instructional Leadership and the Perceptions of the Individuals Involved." *The Bulletin of the National Association of Secondary-School Principals*, 35:83-91, November 1951.
27. COREY, STEPHEN M., and HALVERSON, PAUL M. "The Educational Leader's Ideas about His Interpersonal Relations." *The Bulletin of the National Association of Secondary-School Principals*, 36:57-63, October 1952.
28. COREY, STEPHEN M., HALVERSON, PAUL M., and LOWE, ELIZABETH. *Teachers Prepare for Discussion Group Leadership*. New York, Bureau of Publications, Teachers College, Columbia University, 1953. 34 p.
29. CUNNINGHAM, RUTH, MIEL, ALICE, and ASSOCIATES. *Ways of Working for Curriculum Improvement*. (To be published by the Bureau of Publications, Teachers College, Columbia University, New York.)
30. DAVIS, RONCISCO WILLSON. "An Exploratory Study of Factors Governing the Practical Use of Research Findings in Local School Systems." Ed.D. Project Report. New York, Teachers College, Columbia University, 1952. 94 p. Typewritten.
31. DEWEY, JOHN. *Democracy and Education*. New York, The Macmillan Company, c1916. 434 p.
32. DEWEY, JOHN. *How We Think*. Rev. ed. New York, D. C. Heath and Company, 1933. 301 p.
33. DEWEY, JOHN. *Logic: The Theory of Inquiry*. New York, Henry Holt and Company, c1938. 546 p.
34. DEWEY, JOHN. *The Sources of a Science of Education*. New York, Liveright Publishing Corporation, 1929. 77 p.
35. DOLL, RONALD C., HALVERSON, PAUL M., and LOWE, ELIZABETH. "An Experiment in Training Teachers for Discussion Group Leadership." *Educational Leadership*, 10:112-117, November 1952.
36. DOUGLASS, HARL R. "The Relation of High School Preparation

and Certain Other Factors to Academic Success at the University of Oregon." University of Oregon Publications, Education Series, vol. 3, no. 1. Eugene, Oregon, University of Oregon Press, 1931. 61 p.

37. EVANS, HUBERT M., ed. "Cooperative Research and Curriculum Improvement." *Teachers College Record*, 51:407-474, April 1950.

38. FOSHAY, A. WELLESLEY, and HALL, JAMES A. "Experimentation Moves into the Classroom." *Teachers College Record*, 51:353-359, March 1950.

39. FOSHAY, A. WELLESLEY, WANN, KENNETH D., and ASSOCIATES. *Children's Social Values: An Action Research Study*. (To be published by the Bureau of Publications, Teachers College, Columbia University, New York.)

40. GOOD, CARTER V., BARR, A. S., and SCATES, DOUGLAS E. *The Methodology of Educational Research*. New York, D. Appleton-Century Company, Inc., c1936. 882 p.

41. GWYNN, J. MINOR. *Curriculum Principles and Social Trends*. New York, The Macmillan Company, 1950. 768 p.

42. HALVERSON, PAUL M. "Group Work in Cooperative Curriculum Development." Ed.D. Project Report. New York, Teachers College, Columbia University, 1952. 203 p. Typewritten.

43. HERRICK, VIRGIL E. "The Survey versus the Cooperative Study." *Educational Administration and Supervision*, 34:449-458, December 1948.

44. HOPKINS, L. THOMAS. "Dynamics in Research." *Teachers College Record*, 51:339-346, March 1950.

45. JAHODA, MARIE, DEUTSCH, MORTON, and COOK, STUART W. *Research Methods in Social Relations*. 2 vols. New York, The Dryden Press, c1951. 759 p.

46. JOHNSON, PAUL E. "Patterns of Curriculum Development in Member Schools of the Michigan Secondary-School–College Agreement." Ph.D. Dissertation. Detroit, Wayne University, 1952. 223 p. Typewritten.

47. KNOWLES, MALCOLM S. "Move Over, Mr. Robert." *Adult Leadership*, 1:2-4, June 1952.

48. KOOPMAN, G. ROBERT, MIEL, ALICE, and MISNER, PAUL J. *Democracy in School Administration*. New York, D. Appleton-Century Company, Inc., c1943. 330 p.

49. KRUG, EDWARD A. *Curriculum Planning*. New York, Harper and Brothers, c1950. 306 p.

50. Lawler, Marcella. "Work of the Consultant: Factors That Have Facilitated and Impeded His Work in Selected Elementary Schools of the Horace Mann-Lincoln Institute of School Experimentation." Ed.D. Project Report. New York, Teachers College, Columbia University, 1949. 187 p. Typewritten.
51. Lewin, Kurt. *Resolving Social Conflicts.* New York, Harper and Brothers, c1948. 230 p.
52. Lippitt, Ronald. *Training in Community Relations.* New York, Harper and Brothers, c1949. 286 p.
53. Lippitt, Ronald, and Radke, Marian. "New Trends in the Investigation of Prejudice." *Annals of the American Academy of Political and Social Science,* 244:167-176, March 1946.
54. Liveright, A. A. *Union Leadership Training.* New York, Harper and Brothers, 1951. 265 p.
55. Lowe, Elizabeth. "An Analysis of the Activities of Three Curriculum Committees." Ed.D. Project Report. New York, Teachers College, Columbia University, 1952. 118 p. Typewritten.
56. Lundberg, George A. *Can Science Save Us?* New York, Longmans, Green and Company, 1947. 122 p.
57. Mackenzie, Gordon N., Corey, Stephen M., and associates. *Instructional Leadership.* (To be published by the Bureau of Publications, Teachers College, Columbia University, New York.)
58. Maier, Norman R. F. *Principles of Human Relations.* New York, John Wiley and Sons, Inc., 1952. 474 p.
59. Mann, Floyd C. "Human Relations Skills in Social Research." *Human Relations,* 4, no. 4:341-354, 1951.
60. McNerney, Chester T. *Educational Supervision.* New York, McGraw-Hill Book Company, Inc., 1951. 341 p.
61. Miel, Alice. *Changing the Curriculum: A Social Process.* New York, D. Appleton-Century Company, Inc., c1946. 242 p.
62. Monroe, Walter S., and Engelhart, Max D. *The Scientific Study of Educational Problems.* New York, The Macmillan Company, 1936. 504 p.
63. Mort, Paul R., and Cornell, Francis G. *American Schools in Transition.* New York, Bureau of Publications, Teachers College, Columbia University, 1941. 546 p.
64. Moses, Lincoln E. "Non-parametric Statistics for Psychological Research." *Psychological Bulletin,* 49:123-143, March 1952.
65. Murphy, Gardner, Murphy, Lois Barclay, and Newcomb, Theodore M. *Experimental Social Psychology.* Rev. ed. New York, Harper and Brothers, 1937. 1,121 p.

66. NATIONAL SOCIETY FOR THE STUDY OF EDUCATION. *The Psychology of Learning.* Forty-first Yearbook, Part II. Bloomington, Illinois, Public School Publishing Company, 1942. 463 p.
67. REDEFER, FREDERICK L. "The Eight Year Study—Eight Years Later." Ed.D. Project Report. New York, Teachers College, Columbia University, 1952. 220 p. Typewritten.
68. RICE, J. M. "The Futility of the Spelling Grind." Parts I and II. *The Forum,* 23:163-172, 409-419; April and June 1897.
69. RICE, J. M. *Scientific Management in Education.* New York, Hinds, Noble and Eldridge, 1913. 282 p.
70. ROGERS, CARL R. "Communication: Its Blocking and Its Facilitation." Paper read before the Centennial Conference on Communications, Northwestern University, Evanston, Illinois, October 11, 1951. 9 p. Rexographed.
71. SMITH, B. OTHANEL, STANLEY, WILLIAM O., and SHORES, J. HARLAN. *Fundamentals of Curriculum Development.* New York, World Book Company, c1950. 780 p.
72. SMITH, EUGENE R., TYLER, RALPH W., and the EVALUATION STAFF. *Appraising and Recording Student Progress.* New York, Harper and Brothers, 1942. 550 p.
73. SMITH, MARY NEEL. "Action Research to Improve Teacher Planning Meetings." *The School Review,* 60:142-150, March 1952.
74. SNYGG, DONALD, and COMBS, ARTHUR W. *Individual Behavior.* New York, Harper and Brothers, c1949. 386 p.
75. TABA, HILDA, BRADY, ELIZABETH HALL, and ROBINSON, JOHN T. *Intergroup Education in Public Schools.* Washington, D. C., American Council on Education, c1952. 337 p.
76. TROYER, RAYMOND E. "The Principles of Consultative Work in Education." Ph.D. Dissertation. Chicago, University of Chicago, 1951. 374 p. Typewritten.
77. WANN, KENNETH D. "Teachers as Researchers." *Educational Leadership,* 9:489-495, May 1952.
78. WANN, KENNETH D. "Teacher Participation in Action Research Directed toward Curriculum Change." Ed.D. Project Report. New York, Teachers College, Columbia University, 1950. 240 p. Typewritten.
79. WRIGHTSTONE, J. WAYNE. "Research-Action Programs for Research Bureaus." *Journal of Educational Research,* 42:623-629, April 1949.
80. YAUCH, WILBUR A. *Improving Human Relations in School Administration.* New York, Harper and Brothers, 1949. 299 p.

INDEX

Index

Action research
  attitude of teachers toward, 23, 69 f.
  common sense and, chap. iv
  conditions favorable to, chap. v
  cooperation in, 15 f., 36-40, 95
  definition of, viii, 6
  democracy and, 17, 24
  design of, 12 f., 40 f.
  effect of, on practice, 8 f.
  generalizing from, 13 f., 36 f., 133-139
  history of, 7
  illustrations of, 30-35, 36, chap. iii
  process of, 48, chap. ii
  quality of, 13, 35, 83 f., chap. iv
  sampling problem and, 14, 132 f.
  status leadership and, chap. v
  traditional research and, 8-16, 17 f.
  types of, 42
Adult Leadership, 106
American Educational Research Association, membership of, 4
Anderson, G. Lester, on learning, 22
Axtelle, George A., 24

Banks, Tressa, 61
Barr, A. S., 20
Benne, Kenneth D., 44, 106
  on democracy as science of human relations, 24
  on group tasks, 42
Biographical method
  study of, 61-70
  study of, analyzed, 78-84
Boring, Edwin G., 2
Bradford, Leland P., on hidden agenda, 90
Brady, Elizabeth Hall, 7
Buckingham, Burdette Ross, on research for teachers, 19 f.

Campbell, Clyde M., 44
Cartwright, Dorwin, 22

INDEX

Caswell, Hollis L., 105
  on action research and generalizing, 42
Cattell, J. M., 2
Chamberlain, Dean, 11
Chamberlain, Enid, 11
Chambers, Whittaker, 24
Chein, Isidor, on varieties of action research, 42
Coffman, William E., 105
Collier, John
  on action research, 7
  on cooperative action research and democracy, 17
  on research consultation, 103
Combs, Arthur W., 22
Common sense
  action research and, chap. iv
  method of science and, 85
  problem solving and, 72-78
Consultation, 38 f., 44, 102 f.
Cook, Stuart W., 42, 44
Cooperation
  action research and, 36-40, 95
  need for, in experimentation, 15 f., 24
Corey, Stephen M., 42, 61, 105, 106
Cornell, Francis G., 21
Cunningham, Ruth, 105
Curriculum improvement
  through action research, 23
  cooperative, 90, 95-100
  group morale and, 44

Darwin, Charles, 2
Davis, Roncisco Willson, 23
Decisions, basis for, 26
Deutsch, Morton, 44
Dewey, John, 19, 40
  on common sense and science, 85
  on recency of experimental method, 43
  on reflective thinking, 45
Doll, Ronald C., 106, 140
Douglass, Harl R., 11
Drought, Neal E., 11

Educational goals
  hypotheses and, 27 f.
  relationship among, 28 f., 35
Educational practice
  concern of professional researcher about, 5 f., 8
  methods of changing, 8-12
  relation of knowledge to, 8
  relation of research to, 6, 7
  time required to change, 21
Eight Year Study, 11, 24, 40
Engelhart, Max D., 19, 20
Evans, Hubert M., 39, 41, 106
  on group morale and curricular experimentation, 44
Evidence
  examples of, 54-56, 59, 67-69, 77, 81
  importance of, 26, 100 f.
  objectivity of, 33
  reliability of, 34
  validity of, 34
Experimentation
  control of, 28
  encouragement for, 94
  morale and, 94 f.
  risk involved in, 39
  scientific method of, 2
  time and resources for, 101 f.

Farley, Edgar S., 61
Foshay, A. Wellesley, 23, 44, 106
Freedom to discuss problems
  conditions encouraging, 87-90
  importance for research of, 87

Garrett, H. E., 140
Gates, Arthur I., 22
Generalizing from research, 13-15, 42, 77 f., 81 ff.
  population sampling and, 133 f., 138 f.
Goals, educational
  hypotheses and, 27 ff.
  relationship among, 28 f., 35
Good, Carter V., 20
Gove Junior High School, 47
Group dynamics, 99
Group problem solving, 36-40
Group work
  improvement in, 95-100
  training in, 99 f.
Gwynn, J. Minor, 105

Hall, James A., 44
Halverson, Paul M., 105, 106
Harding, John, 42
Herrick, Virgil E., 7
Hopkins, L. Thomas, on research, 21
Horace Mann-Lincoln Institute of School Experimentation
  Battle Creek Study and, 61
  cooperative research and, 95
  Leadership Studies, 47, 105
  policy of, x, 25, 86
  seminar, chap. vi
Hypotheses, 9, 12 f., 27, 36, 75 f.
  feasibility of, 37
  motivation for, 27
  nature of, 27 f.
  as prediction, 27
  relation of goals to, 28, 30
  sources of, 30
  testing of, examples, 5 f., 51 f., 62 ff., 75 f., 79 f., 134-138

"Ideas about Myself" (questionnaire), 110, 112 f., 124
Invention, opportunities for, 91-93

Jahoda, Marie, 44
Johnson, Paul E., 23

Knowles, Malcolm S., 106
Knowledge, as related to action, 8, 22
Koopman, G. Robert, 44, 105
Krug, Edward A., 106

Lawler, Marcella, 44, 105
Leadership techniques, illustrative study of, 30-36
Learning
  action research and, chap. vi
  nature of, 8 f., 22
Lewin, Kurt, 7, 21
Lippitt, Ronald, 43
  on consequences of research in physical and human sciences, 23
  on cooperation in research, 16, 21
Liveright, A. A., 106
Lowe, Elizabeth, 105, 106
Lundberg, George A., on science in practical affairs, 43

Mackenzie, Gordon N., 25, 42, 105, 106
Maier, Norman R. F., 106
Mann, Floyd C., 44
McNerney, Chester T., 106
Measurement of committee productivity, 32 ff.
Michigan Secondary-School—College Agreement, 12, 23

Miel, Alice, 44, 105, 106
Misner, Paul J., 44, 105 f.
Monroe, Walter S.
  on difference between researchers and practitioners, 20 f.
  on science of education, 19
Mort, Paul R., on time-diffusion patterns for school innovations, 21
Moses, Lincoln E., 23
Muntyan, Bozidar, 44, 106
Murphy, Gardner, on group thinking, 38
Murphy, Lois Barclay, 38

Newcomb, Theodore M., 38

Operations research, 22

Permissive atmosphere, importance of, for curricular experimentation, 90, 92
Powers, Oscar, 61
Problem definition, 75, 78 f.
Problem solving
  action research and, 78-84
  common sense and, 72-78
  groups and, 36-40
  as learning, 22
Productivity of committees
  definition of, 33
  measurement of, 32 ff.
Psychological research in America, 2

Radke, Marian, 43
Raup, Bruce, 24
Redefer, Frederick L., on Eight Year Study, 11, 24, 40
Reflective thinking, 45
Research findings, school practices and, 11 f.

Rice, J. M., on the science of education, 19
Robinson, John T., 7
Rogers, Carl R., on understanding an opponent, 92
Role-playing, as learning method, 113-118

Scates, Douglas E., 20
Scientific method
  distinguished from common sense, 71 f., 85
  function of, in education, 4 f., 6
  practical problems and, 43, 71
  relativity of, 18
Scientific movement in education, 1 ff., 19
  practical problems and, 43
Sheats, Paul, 42
Shores, J. Harlan, 106
Smith, B. Othanel, 24, 106
Smith, Eugene R., 21
Smith, Mary Neel, 47
Snygg, Donald, 22
Stanley, William O., 106
Statistics
  basic concepts of, for action research, 130 ff.
  effects of instruction in, 126-129
  relation of, to practical problems, 127 ff.
  scope of instruction in, 128 f.
Status leadership
  action research and, 87 ff., 94 f., 96 f.
  in-service education and, 105

Taba, Hilda, 7
Teachers
  attitude of, toward action research, 23, 69 f.

Teachers—*continued*
  improvement of planning by, 47-61
  research by, 3 f., 19 ff.
  study of biographical method by, 61-70
Theory, as source of hypotheses, 30
Traditional educational research, 1-6
  design of, 12
  distinguished from action research, 8-16
  effect of, on practice, 8 f.
  generalizing from, 13
  method of, 4 f., 12, 28
  purpose of, 4
  value of, 13
Troyer, Raymond E., 44
Tyler, Ralph W., 21

Vandermeer, Floyd, 61

Waldorf, Robert, 61
Wann, Kenneth D., 23, 105, 106
Waskin, L. S., 23
Wrightstone, J. Wayne, 7, 140

Yauch, Wilbur A., 44